O.C. Stubb

Nashville, Tenn.

Feb. 7, 1949

SOVIET RUSSIA

An Introduction

THE ROYAL INSTITUTE
OF INTERNATIONAL AFFAIRS
London: Chatham House, St James's Square, S.W.1.
New York: 542 Fifth Avenue, New York 19, N.Y.

Toronto   Bombay
Melbourne   Cape Town
OXFORD UNIVERSITY PRESS

SOVIET RUSSIA
An Introduction

by

KATHLEEN GIBBERD

REVISED EDITION

LONDON & NEW YORK
Royal Institute
of International Affairs

A*

First published February 1942
Reprinted April 1942
Reprinted June 1942
Reprinted October 1942
Reprinted March 1943
Revised edition 1946

PRINTED IN GREAT BRITAIN
AT THE BROADWATER PRESS, WELWYN GARDEN CITY
HERTFORDSHIRE

CONTENTS

PREFACE

MR H. G. WELLS, when he visited Moscow in 1920, referred to Soviet Russia as "this dark crystal." After twenty-six years the description is still appropriate. The chaos that was visible in 1920 has long disappeared, but once the new regime emerged from civil war and began to take shape and form, a cloud of obscurity dimmed its features for the outside world. This was to some extent inevitable, since the outside world had no experience to help it recognize the significance of events that were the outcome of a new and revolutionary political doctrine. But the obscurity was also due to the entirely contradictory reports that foreign observers brought back to their own countries—and perhaps this was also inevitable as very few visited the U.S.S.R. for the idle pleasure of foreign travel and nearly all took with them either a predisposition to admire or an instinctive distrust. Yet again, there was a certain withdrawal from the rest of the world on the part of Russia herself. Soviet citizens were mostly debarred from travel abroad and knew little about conditions beyond their frontiers, while the Soviet Government was unwilling to allow any foreigner investigations in the interior of the country. The lack of accurate information as between the U.S.S.R. and other countries was thus mutual.

This book was originally undertaken at the request of lecturers engaged in Army education, and is therefore primarily intended for men and women who wish to know something of the internal conditions of a country that has become so powerful an ally. In the four years that have passed since the first edition, a great deal of information about the U.S.S.R. has been disseminated in this country. As a result it has been possible to establish as facts certain things which were there set down as probabilities. Four years have also changed the perspective and made it advisable to omit some passages as no longer relevant. Although the war itself still remains outside the compass of this book, it has been necessary to add some changes of a permanent nature that have been introduced into the Soviet regime during the war years. Also, the section on the Red Army has been expanded and a new chapter has been added summarizing Soviet foreign relations in Europe before the war and Soviet foreign relations in general down to the San Francisco Conference.

There are necessarily some important omissions. It was not possible, for instance, within so small a compass to do justice either to the range of Soviet scientific research, or to the vitality of the arts in present-day Russia and their widespread appreciation among the people. While, however, the picture is necessarily incomplete, every effort has been made to arrive at accuracy.

K. G.

10

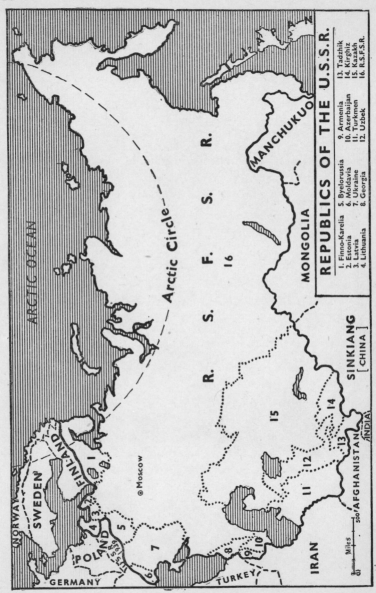

THE REPUBLICS OF THE U.S.S.R.

REPUBLICS OF THE U.S.S.R.

1. Finno-Karelia	5. Byelorussia	9. Armenia	13. Tadzhik
2. Estonia	6. Moldavia	10. Azerbaijan	14. Kirghiz
3. Latvia	7. Ukraine	11. Turkmen	15. Kazakh
4. Lithuania	8. Georgia	12. Uzbek	16. R.S.F.S.R.

I

TERRITORIES AND PEOPLES

THE general geography of Russia is very easy to keep in mind, for the greater part of the country is one vast plain that takes on a changing appearance as one proceeds away from the North Pole and towards the Equator. In the extreme north, and extending southward for a varying distance, is the bleak expanse of the "tundra," a land of rocks, scrub, and marshy hollows, with the earth permanently frozen a few feet below the surface. South of this is the largest belt of forest in the world, covering half the total area of the U.S.S.R. In European Russia the trees begin north of Archangel, but away to the east, where the climate is more severe, the tundra reaches further south. At first the forest is a dark mass of pines and firs, but as one moves southwards, other trees appear, and the forest thins out into open spaces. Further south still, the trees disappear altogether, and we come to the famous steppe country—a great expanse of treeless, rolling plain, more fertile than any other region of the world. This "black earth" extends from Eastern Ukraine beyond the Urals into Siberia. East of the Caspian fertility has gone, and the steppe has turned to desert.

The Russian plain ends in mountains in the east and south, the best known ranges being the Pamirs, the "roof of the world," which are partly in Afghanistan and separate Russia from India, the Altai Mountains in Siberia, and the Caucasus, between the Black and Caspian Seas. Interrupting the plain in a long line that extends from north to south, almost from the Arctic Ocean to the Caspian, are the Urals—a range of wooded hills not so high as the Lakeland fells of Cumberland and the traditional boundary between European and Asiatic Russia. Across the plain in a northerly or southerly direction, flow Russia's magnificent rivers; the Dniester and the Dnieper into the Black Sea, the Don into the Sea of Azov, the Volga into the Caspian. And flowing northwards are the Dvina into the White Sea, and the great Siberian rivers, the Ob, the Yenisei, and the Lena, which have their outlets in the Arctic Ocean. In the Far East is the Amur flowing into the Pacific. These and other rivers, with their tributaries, make up a system of waterways which, although frozen in winter, have been used for travel and traffic through immemorial summers.

So large a country naturally contains a variety of peoples; the population, in fact, includes something like sixty different nationalities. By far the largest number of these are the Russians themselves, who make up nearly three-quarters of the whole and are chiefly found in the heart of European Russia. In the course of history Russian rulers extended their authority over neighbouring territories so that Russia proper came to be almost encircled by dependent provinces inhabited, for the most part, by non-Russian peoples. In the west these border States were relatively small, but the regions acquired in the east amounted to one-third of the continent of Asia. The whole formerly constituted the Russian Empire of the Tsars and was ruled authoritatively, and not without oppression, from the former capital, St Petersburg (afterwards re-named Petrograd, and later Leningrad). Nowadays the one-time Empire has become the Union of Soviet Socialist Republics and a new kind of direction and control comes from the new capital, Moscow. In this chapter we are not concerned with new methods of government, but with that diversity of lands and people which enriches the Soviet Union as it once enriched the Empire of the Tsars. In order to get some clear impression of this diversity, let us suppose that an imaginary aerial journey be taken round the borderlands of the U.S.S.R. If we begin in the far north and travel over the European frontier States to the Caucasus, then turn eastwards into Asia, then north-east as far as the Pacific, and finally return through Siberia to Moscow, we shall traverse every constituent State of the Union.

THE EUROPEAN REPUBLICS [1]

The northernmost part of Russia is not far from the North Pole, and starting from these regions of perpetual ice and prolonged darkness it is likely that the first signs of human life to be observed would be the lonely stations of Soviet explorers—the orange tents of a scientific expedition encamped on an ice floe, and on the desolate mainland a lighthouse to aid the Soviet fleet of icebreakers. By means of these wide-beamed ships which force their passage through frozen seas the Soviets now claim to have opened the northern passage from the Atlantic to the Pacific. In the extreme north-west of European Russia the Lapps—a people of short stature, with high cheek-bones and weather-beaten complexion—eke out a scant living. In summer they may be seen fishing on lonely shores, but their chief occupation is the care and breeding of reindeer, the only animals that can live on the tundra moss. The traditional homes of the Lapps are the primitive constructions of reindeer skins that can be taken down and

[1] In the sketch of European Russia given here the direct effects of the war have not been taken into account. It should be remembered that nearly all the territories described include areas that have been devastated by battle.

B

put up again as the reindeer move on to fresh pasturage, but it is now the policy of the Soviet Government to encourage the Lapps into a more settled life in wooden huts—a policy which some thought doubtful of success, since the Lapps, like all nomadic tribes, do not readily thrive in a settled life.

South of Lapland are the most recent additions to the republics of the Soviet Union: the Finno-Karelian Republic and the Baltic States of Estonia, Latvia and Lithuania. These were all part of the Tsarist Empire. The Finno-Karelian Republic was established after the short war between Russia and Finland in the winter of 1939-40. Russia had demanded the restoration of former Russian naval bases and of territory adjoining the Russian province of Karelia. When Finland finally yielded to these demands the new republic was established in a region that was partly a new acquisition and partly a former Soviet province. Like the people of independent Finland, the inhabitants live a hard life among forests and lakes, making the most of a short summer.

The life of the people in the Baltic States is similar to that of the Finns, the timber trade and agriculture providing the main occupations. Autumn begins in August and the first snows often fall before the threshing is done. The Estonians, the Letts, and the Lithuanians are distinct in appearance from one another, and each has a noticeably different language. There are religious differences also, the Estonians and Letts being mainly Protestant, and the Lithuanians Catholic. For a long period before the last war all the Baltic countries were dominated by the "Baltic barons" who were powerful German landowners. Memories of this domination were doubtless a factor in favour of the Soviet Union when, in the summer of 1940, the Soviet Government sought to make them once again a part of Russia. In the difficult circumstances of the time, it would seem that after their short period of independence they had to come under the authority of either Russia or Germany.

Between Russia and Northern Poland is the Soviet Republic of White Russia (or Byelorussia) which was enlarged by the occupation of Eastern Poland in 1939. The name has no connection with the defenders and exiles of the Tsarist regime, who called themselves "White" in opposition to the Red emblems of the Bolsheviks. The White Russians have always been so called to distinguish them from the main branch of the Russian race. A large part of Byelorussia is flat marshland with tall reeds and clusters of willows. Crops have always been poor and life precarious, and the peasants in their wooden hovels have been the constant victims of fevers. The draining of the land has been accelerated by the Soviet Government, who claim that very soon the greater part of this marshland will be recovered and that already there are many acres planted with rye and potatoes where once there were impassable swamps.

South of White Russia are the Republics of Ukraine and of Moldavia. Moldavia is a small State largely made up of the province of Bessarabia which Russia had lost to Rumania in 1917 and which was only regained in 1940. Ukraine occupies most of Southern European Russia, and, with the addition of Polish Ukraine, is twice the size of Great Britain. Almost the whole country is fertile steppe where grain can be sown year after year without the soil losing its virtue. In June the Ukraine landscape appears like a sea of ripening grain interspersed with patches of yellow and black where sunflowers are grown for the oil from their seeds. Everything grows rapidly in this black earth and grass grown for hay may rise higher than a man's head. Formerly crops were sown in small patches and marked off by divisions that showed where one peasant's strip ended and another's began. Now, under the collective farm system, which here as everywhere else in the U.S.S.R. has combined the farms into large co-operative units, the proprietary divisions have largely disappeared. With no hills or trees to break their force, winds sweep like waves over the Ukraine steppe: burning winds in summer coming from the deserts in the east, and in winter icy cold winds that tear over the snow and make the peasants seal their windows and crowd round the stoves. Not only does Ukraine hold some of the U.S.S.R.'s richest grainland, but the coal mines and iron mines in Eastern Ukraine have made this region the chief industrial area of the Soviet Union. This position is now beginning to be rivalled, however, by new developments in the Urals and in Asiatic Russia.

Ukraine reaches southward to the northern shores of the Black Sea and the smaller adjacent Sea of Azov. Here are important ports: Odessa, where grain for export is loaded; Nikolaev, which is growing in importance as a shipbuilding centre; Sevastopol, on the Crimean peninsula, the chief naval base of the south; and to the east, beyond the borders of Ukraine, are Rostov, the natural exit for the products of the Donetz industrial area, and Batum the oil port. At such places cranes and dockyards, smoke and commercial buildings intrude on the gentle air of relaxation which is otherwise the characteristic of these pleasant shores. Away from these distractions the coast is fringed with palm trees and orange groves, and provides holiday resorts for Soviet workers from all over Russia. The white mansions of dispossessed noblemen of the old regime have become holiday homes, and newly constructed concrete buildings designed for the same purpose stand beside them.

At the eastern end of the Black Sea is a block of land, some 300 miles wide, separating it from the Caspian. Across this, from sea to sea, stretch the Caucasus mountains, a range more beautiful perhaps than any in Europe. Immediately to the south of the main range is the Soviet Republic of Georgia. Tiflis the capital, lying under the steep slopes of the mountains, has always been a city of gaiety and ease, and peopled by a mixture of races. In spite of the new blocks of Soviet buildings and other signs of modern development, its essential character remains. Hawkers from the Near East bring their goods for sale; Turks, Armenians and Persians sit in the open air drinking Caucasian wine. Further south, tracks wind up and over other highlands to Soviet Armenia, a vast and lonely plateau rising sometimes to mountain peaks and broken by deep and magnificent ravines. In the long stretches of undulating grassland red cattle, grey sheep, and the wild-looking horses of the Armenian shepherds seem to be the only living things, until one of the tall mountaineers is seen against the sky-line, or the land dips down to a river with a cluster of brown stone houses and a curious ornate church on its banks. Armenia is a gateway into the Middle East and has been fought for and fought over for centuries. Once it was an independent kingdom, and although afterwards divided up among the neighbouring empires of Persia, Turkey and Russia, it never ceased to trouble its conquerors, and clung tenaciously to its ancient form of Christianity.

East of Armenia, bordering the western shores of the Caspian Sea, is the small Soviet Republic of Azerbaijan, a land of vineyards and cotton fields, and peopled by an Asiatic race who are mostly Mohammedans. Its capital, Baku, lies among a drab expanse of oilfields, oil workers' settlements and docks, but although chiefly renowned as the richest oil-producing

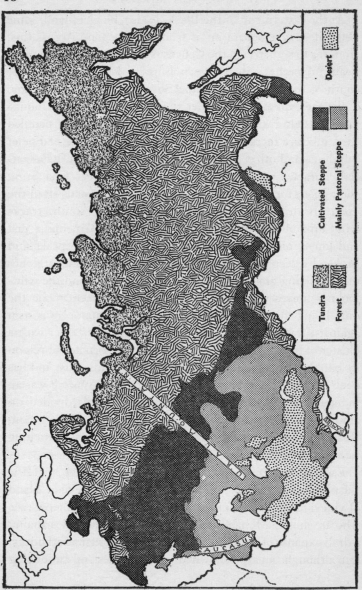

THE U.S.S.R. VEGETATION

Legend:
- Tundra
- Forest
- Cultivated Steppe
- Mainly Pastoral Steppe
- Desert

CAUCASUS

centre in the U.S.S.R. Baku is also a pleasure resort.

SOVIET ASIA

In Transcaucasia—the general name given to the Republics of Georgia, Armenia and Azerbaijan—European and Asiatic Russia are interlocked. If we now cross the Caspian Sea we leave European Russia finally behind. Here is an immense inland region where rivers fail to find the sea and peter away in desert sand. Formerly known as Russian Turkestan, it is now more commonly called Soviet Central Asia; it includes the five republics of the Turkmens, Uzbeks, Tadzhiks, Kirghiz, and Kazaks. As part of the Tsarist Empire, these States provided a route from Russia to Persia, India and China, and brought wealth to cotton planters who came to make their fortunes. The native peoples were mainly left to themselves, and, except that slave trading was suppressed, life was much as it had been since the fourteenth century, when Tamerlane the Great, the Tartar conqueror, established himself among the gilded mosques and blue-tiled Moslem colleges of Samarkand. Across the deserts rode the Turkmens on their camels, a tall, forbidding race, ready for fight and plunder. On the grassy plains and highlands lived the Kirghiz and Kazak herdsmen, shorter, stouter, with legs bowed from a life on horseback. Among the cotton plantations were the clay houses of the Uzbeks, whose women went always veiled, and nearer the Afghan border, on the slopes of the Pamir mountains, lived the bearded Tadzhiks, fanatical Moslems yet haunted by old superstitions. In the old cities of Taskhent, Bokhara, and Samarkand all races mingled, presenting a dazzling spectacle in the hot sunlight—turbaned men in coloured robes; women in baggy trousers with jingling ornaments; carpet vendors, squatting among their hanging rugs; camels and donkeys with bells and ornate harness; sherbet sellers clinking their glasses; Moslem mullahs preoccupied in meditation; and among them all the ever-present oriental beggar displaying his sores and deformities.

All this is changing under Soviet rule. The spectacle is probably still much the same, but with portraits of Lenin and Stalin, Communist posters, propagandist cinemas and loud-speakers introduced into the Eastern scene. Private trade is decreasing, and the bazaars are coming under collective ownership. The rich men and the native chiefs now have no place and women are encouraged to go unveiled.

We have now travelled over all but one of the sixteen constituent republics of the Soviet Union, and the remaining expanse of Russian territory, although containing various provinces that have limited self-government, is part of Russia proper, or to give it its proper title, the Russian Soviet Federated Socialist Republic. As the map on page 10 shows, the R.S.F.S.R. includes not only all of European Russia from the western border States of the Urals, but also the immense stretch of land east of the Urals. This reaches as far as the Pacific and is bounded on the north by the Arctic Ocean and on the south by Sinkiang and Outer Mongolia (both under Soviet influence) and by the Chinese province of Manchuria; it is still customary to call it by the general name of Siberia, although this properly now applies only to part of it. It is sparsely inhabited, and although dotted about with growing industrial centres, as well as with agricultural areas, some of which have been newly put under cultivation, it must still be regarded as largely undeveloped. In this rapid survey we can do no more than cover it swiftly.

Proceeding, then, in a north-easterly direction from Kazakhstan, we travel over the mountainous region between Rus-

sia and China to the Pacific Ocean. Turning north to follow
the coastal area of the Russian Far East, we come to a magnificent land of high mountains and largely unexplored
forests, where trees and flowers that normally are separated by
warmer and colder climates grow in profusion together and
where tigers prowl through the undergrowth. The coast itself
is scattered with fishing villages, and small settlements of
strange and primitive tribes appear in clearings in the forest.
At the southern end of this territory is Vladivostock, the
eastern terminus of the Trans-Siberian Railway and separated from Japan by a few hundred miles of sea. In the extreme north the northernmost icy finger of Soviet territory
closely approaches the northernmost point of Alaska, which is
part of the United States, and, in fact, the distance between
them is only about three times that between Dover and Cal-
ais. We will not, however, travel so far north, but having followed the coastline until it bends southwards to form the
volcanic peninsula of Kamchatka turn abruptly west and
make for Moscow.

For 2,000 miles we cross the tundra and pine forests of
Yakutia, an area twenty times the size of England and Wales.
The Yakuts, who number about 400,000, are one of the most
outstanding of the peoples of Eastern Russia, chiefly because
of their aptitude for imitating the west. Their simple dwellings of rough logs or of skins, their superstitious belief in
spirits and their traditional occupations of trapping and hunt-
ing suggest a comparison with the North American Indians.
But unlike the latter they have not declined as the result of
impact with civilization. On the contrary, their population
increases, and they have learnt to become herdsmen and
agriculturists, and have developed astuteness in commercial
dealings.

Southward from Yakutia are Eastern and Western Siberia, a land of forests in the north and of fertile plains in the south. These provinces and the territory that formerly went under the general name of Siberia are still, as in Tsarist days, a destination for political prisoners. Under the Tsars the enemies of the autocracy were allowed a good deal of freedom once they had been safely removed beyond the Urals. Indeed, many of those who helped to mould the present Soviet system spent years of study in the rough wooden huts of Siberia, occasionally putting aside the writings of Marx and Engels to hunt fish or play chess with neighbouring exiles. Nowadays, the prisoners chiefly work in lumber camps, sleeping in barracks that are not very different from those of the voluntary workers who, in the summer season, make their way to the new settlements on the Siberian rivers, where the felled trees arrive in long floating lines and are hauled ashore to feed the saw mills. Life in these remote places is now often varied by State-provided entertainments and propagandist lectures.

The further westward we go the less rigorous does the climate become, for there are no high mountains in Eastern Europe to interrupt the temperate winds from the Atlantic. We therefore find the mid-Urals a pleasant land of wooded hills and pastures. Beyond them, we cross the higher reaches of the Volga, most famous of Russia's rivers and a waterway that has lured adventurers and emigrants through the ages, many of them to make small permanent settlements on its banks. Among the best known of these Volga communities were the Volga Germans and the Volga Cossacks. The former were German settlers brought over by Catherine the Great, who was a German princess. Although they survived as a partly self-governing community under the Soviets they were evacuated by the Russian Government after the German in-

vasion. The Volga Cossacks, like the more famous Cossacks
of the Don, were farming communities that under the Tsars
enjoyed considerable independence in return for their services as cavalrymen in the Tsar's army. They wore a distinc-
tive dress with a large hat and long wide-skirted coat and were
accounted by themselves and others as superior to the ordinary peasants. Their origin goes far back into history when
bands of freelance Russians constituted themselves as fron-
tiersmen against invaders from Asia—the name signifies "free
adventurers." Freedom and independence have always been
the dominant note of Cossack life, and to escape interference
under the Tsarist regime some of them migrated to Siberia,
where they became a civilizing influence. Of these, some later
moved into Manchuria to escape the Soviets, with whom
there was often serious conflict over the collectivization of
the farms.

In travelling over the Far Eastern territories, through
Yakutia and Siberia and the Urals, we have passed without
comment many new industrial centres that seem curious and
defiant intrusions in a world where the forces of nature are
predominant. Now, however, as we approach Moscow, industry seems the more important—factory chimneys and high
concrete buildings are the salient features of the landscape
and the fields and woodlands seem subordinate to them. Thus
we arrive at Moscow itself, capital of this immense Union of
Soviet States. Its wooden houses have largely been replaced
by concrete blocks and its cobbled pavements by asphalt.
New streets have been constructed and an underground railway and trolley buses help to transport the four million
people who have established their right to live in the crowded
city, for no one can live in Moscow without a permit. In the
centre of the city, standing on a hill, is the Kremlin. This

one-time fortress covers one hundred acres, and its various buildings are surrounded by a high battlemented wall with nineteen towers and pierced by five gates. Here is the home of the Soviet Government.

II

THE COLLAPSE OF TSARIST RUSSIA AND THE BUILDING OF THE SOVIET STATE

IT IS difficult in a country like Britain that has had a parliament for six hundred years, where every one is accustomed openly to criticize the Government, and where a secret police is unknown, to throw one's imagination into the Russia of the later nineteenth and early twentieth century. Here was a nation that played an important part in world affairs, a nation that was civilized in the sense that it had old-established universities and had produced from its imaginative and naturally intellectual people writers and thinkers who were famous all over Europe. Yet it was socially backward, had never known free speech, and had never arrived at a satisfactory form of government. The reasons for this are doubtless to be found partly in the Russian temperament, but the earlier history of Russia also helps to explain it. At the time when the rest of Europe was beginning to emerge from the Middle Ages, hordes of Mongol barbarians (the Tartars) invaded Russia from the east, and over-ran the various principalities of which Russia was then composed. For two hundred years the Russian people were held in subjection and progress was at a standstill. When eventually the Mongol Empire began to break up and the Tartars began to retire to the east, they left, according to some historians, a legacy of eastern fatalism, a tendency to inertia and postponement. They also left a Russia divided within itself where rival princes struggled for supremacy. After long and bitter warfare the Grand Dukes of Moscow established their authority and became the absolute rulers of the whole country.

RUSSIA UNDER THE TSARS

The first Moscow Prince to assume the title of Tsar was Ivan the Terrible (formally crowned in 1547), and it is he who is generally considered to have founded the Russian State after the merciless removal of rival princes. But the country remained largely mediaeval in character and removed from western influence until the reign of Peter the Great (1682-1725). The changes brought about by this Tsar were almost as sweeping as those introduced by the Bolsheviks two hundred years later, and were in some respects similar both in object and method. Peter the Great sought to establish the principle of universal service to the State. He worked for the development of Russian industry on western lines, and created a great number of officials to enable him to carry out these and other ideas. He was convinced that all he did was ultimately for the good of Russia and the severe hardships involved in the changes he brought about were, in his view, justified by the ends he had in mind. It is interesting to note that Peter compelled the peasants to work for the boyars (landowners) in order that the boyars might in their turn render proper service to the State. Under later rulers the boyars contracted out of their obligation but continued to make exacting demands of the peasants. Thus the free peasantry became serfs, their property and their labour being in the possession of their masters. Catherine the Great (1762-1796), who was the next most notable ruler, did nothing to better the condition of the serfs although, like Peter the Great, she tried to westernize the country. She repudiated, however, the ideas of the French Revolution which were popular among certain sections of the people. At the beginning of the nineteenth century the first beginnings of democratic government were planned by Tsar Alexander I, but before they took form Russia was involved in the Napoleonic Wars. By a curious irony Russia, the most backward of the Powers that resisted Napoleon, was finally responsible for his downfall. After conquering most of Europe Napoleon invaded Russia in 1812 and reached Moscow after that city had been burnt by the retreating Russians. Forced to turn back, Napoleon lost five-sixths of his army in the retreat, and with them went the legend of invincibility and success which his former triumphs had bequeathed to him.

In the hundred years between the Napoleonic wars and the Great War of 1914, various reforms were introduced into Russia, but changes came slowly and the traditional autocratic power of the Tsar remained unimpaired. In 1861, after long pressure from groups of intellectuals and liberal-minded aristocrats such as Count Tolstoy, serfdom was abolished; but conditions were not greatly improved, for the heavy payments and restrictions imposed on the emancipated serfs forced many of them to return to the landowners as hired labourers. In 1905, when revolutionary strikes followed defeat in the war with Japan, a Duma, or parliament, was granted for the first time; but far from being the representative and sovereign authority that the word conveys to British ears, it was elected by only a proportion of the people, and it had no control over the Ministers of State, still less over the Tsar. It became, however, the voice of liberal and progressive opinion, and the country councils (zemstvos) which had been granted earlier served the same purpose. Although the Tsar was traditionally called the "little father" of the Russian people his absolute authority was considered by all reformers as an obstacle to progress. Indeed, certain revolutionary groups made the assassination of the ruler their first purpose, and each succeeding monarch went in constant danger of his life. To protect himself against such internal enemies, the Tsar relied on his personal soldiery and on an elaborate network of secret police. These agents of the Throne were constantly rounding up conspirators and bringing them to trial. Imprisonment or a sentence of exile in Siberia usually followed.

THE BOLSHEVIK REVOLUTION

It was in these conditions that the man who was ultimately to become the first leader of a revolutionary Russia grew up. Vladimir Ilytch Ulyanov, afterwards known as Lenin, was the son of a school inspector and younger brother to one of the revolutionaries who was hanged as an accomplice in the murder of Tsar Alexander II. Beginning life in a mixture of moderate material comfort and revolutionary talk, he went from school to university, but in his first term was expelled for showing revolutionary tendency. It was in the leisure time that he then had at his disposal that he began his study of Marx, and the study continued for twenty years, aided rather than interrupted by periods of imprisonment and exile. As a leading member of the newly constituted and illegal Russian Social Democratic Party he was continually under suspicion, and frequently tried and convicted. It was while he was in Siberia that Lenin married a fellow revolutionary who was also serving a term of exile and who thenceforward became a partner in all his revolutionary work. For some time Lenin worked as a lawyer, but later, in order to avoid the secret police, he left Russia. In long years, living in modest lodgings in Geneva and London, he developed and applied Marxist ideas in the light of his own knowledge and experience.

While in full agreement with Marx that the wage-earners

would at some future date be forced to rise in revolution against the Capitalists, Lenin became nevertheless convinced that the revolution would fail unless it was directed by a section of the workers who were aware of what was happening, and who would, in fact, seize the flood tide when it came and launch the ship of socialism. He determined, therefore, to make the Russian Social Democratic Party into a select, disciplined band of professional revolutionaries, primarily wage-earners, who should prepare themselves for the event. At the second Congress of the Russian Social Democrats in 1903 he fought for this opinion against those who were inclined to increase the membership of the party by allowing all sympathizers to join it regardless of their exact shades of opinion, their willingness to act, or social origin. The Congress would have been illegal in Russia and was, therefore, summoned to Brussels, but as the Belgian police made difficulties, it moved to London, where an obliging British business man, feeling sorry for the collection of harmless Russians who were not allowed to talk over their grievances in their own country, offered to pay for the hiring of a hall. The Congress was a crucial one, and Lenin's view in favour of a small disciplined party prevailed by a narrow majority. A split among the Social Democrats resulted, and henceforward there were two parties instead of one. They came to be known as the Bolsheviks and the Mensheviks—the names meaning the majority and the minority. Each continued to work according to its own beliefs, the Mensheviks being willing to incorporate all sympathizers in their ranks, the Bolsheviks being a smaller and more disciplined body.

It was the Great War that finally made the collapse of the old regime inevitable. The Russian soldiers fought with extreme courage against the Germans, despite a growing lack

C

of munitions and the absence of properly equipped field
hospitals. Men seized guns from dying comrades; surgical
operations were performed without anaesthetics. But at home
things went badly. The weak Tsar had gone to army headquarters, and the Empress who ruled in his place under the
guidance of Rasputin—a supposed holy man who successfully concealed his unpleasant private life from the Royal
Family and became their friend and counsellor—was determined above all things to maintain the autocratic power of the
throne. Rasputin's assassination came too late to save the regime. The old order finally broke up of itself. Every one knew
that something must happen. Machine-guns had been placed
by Government orders among the roofs and towers of Petrograd. Some said that the secret police had been instructed to
provoke a riot which would then be suppressed so ruthlessly
that it would discourage any further revolutionary activity.
During a week-end in March 1917, a small crowd collected in
Petrograd and smashed some bakers' shops—there was a
bread shortage, although it was officially declared that there
was plenty of bread in the city. Factories stopped work, and
the employees poured out into the streets. People said that
the revolution had come and seemed to be waiting for it to
happen. Soldiers appeared, marching in formation, with orders
to disperse the people. They fired a few aimless shots and then
joined the populace. Other soldiers broke barracks and came
up offering their rifles to any one who would like to have them
and embracing those who took them. "For the people or
against the people?" the soldiers asked each other as they met
in the crowds; and in the evening small boys were shooting
pigeons with Guardsmen's rifles.

In the Parliament House the members of the Duma hastily
met, deciding that it was their responsibility to deal with the

crisis and that they must appoint a Government from among themselves. It was imperative that the Tsar should abdicate and the new Provisional Government sent an urgent request that he should do so. The Tsar had at first sent troops against Petrograd from his army headquarters, but these soldiers never arrived, and being finally persuaded that he had no adequate following in the country, Nicholas II abdicated in favour of his brother. The nomination, however, was not acceptable, and Tsardom went for ever.

The Provisional Government was determined to act for "the people" and tried to make itself representative of all progressive forces from the more humanitarian conservatives to the peasant labour party whose leader was Kerensky. Kerensky came to join the Provisional Government—and ultimately to lead it—from a rival body that was meeting elsewhere in the city. This was the Petrograd Soviet, a hastily constituted council of soldiers and workers elected from barracks and factories. (At the time of the abortive General Strike in 1905 the strike committees, chosen to represent the dissatisfied workpeople, had been called "soviets"—meaning councils or committees—and the term had come to stand for any elected body of revolutionary workers or soldiers.) At first there was some agreed division of powers by which the Provisional Government made decrees that had to be submitted to the Soviet for its approval before being proclaimed. However, as time went on the Soviet became the stronger body and was supported by similar soviets of soldiers and workers throughout the country. Soon nearly every town, every factory of importance and every regimental unit had its soviet.

In the meantime Lenin, who was in Switzerland at the time of the Revolution, contrived, with German aid, to get back to Russia where he was joined by Leon Trotsky, formerly a Menshevik but now a Bolshevik, and chiefly useful as a soldier and for his gift of powerful oratory. Lenin had by now a small but highly efficient Bolshevik following and those united and disciplined revolutionaries gradually obtained a majority in the soviets, including the Central Soviet in Petrograd. When ultimately a final clash came with the Provisional Government, which was accused of delaying its promised reforms and scheming to restore the autocracy, the soviets easily won, for whereas the Provisional Government was made up of various opinions and was a compromise between the old and the new, the soviets represented the revolutionary workers and were directed by professional revolutionaries who knew precisely what they wanted and were prepared at all costs to carry it out. Thus came the Second Revolution in November 1917, heralding the Socialist or Communist State. The Bolsheviks, or Communists as they were soon to be called, immediately began to build up their own administration machine. Private ownership in industry was abolished and the first signs of the change were the control of the factories by the workers and the seizure of the land by the peasants. But these, as will be seen, were temporary measures more in the nature of a celebration of the proletarian victory than the foundation stones of the new State, for the Communist programme did not permit of mob rule. The first important act of the new Soviet Government (so-called because it claimed that it derived its authority from the people's soviets) was to conclude the war with Germany. Unlike all the other revolutionary parties in Russia, the Bolsheviks had from the outset condemned the war as a struggle for power between capitalist countries. Now Russia's part in it was brought to an end by the Treaty of Brest-Litovsk, negotiated with the Germans by Trotsky. It was a humiliating peace that would have meant the loss of all Russia's western provinces, including the rich land of Ukraine, had not the victory of the Allies a few months later made it null and void. It shook the prestige of Lenin, for, weary of war as were all Russian soldiers and civilians, they had not yet quite forgotten the patriotic fire which swept over their country in 1914. However, Lenin was not greatly troubled by the price of peace, for he was convinced that the revolution which had begun in Russia would soon break out all over Europe. His Communist Party was linked with other revolutionary parties in other States, and he looked forward to their early assembly in a new International to which they would bring tidings of world revolution. In this, however, he was mistaken, for although the Communist International met periodically in the years that followed, it was never able to acclaim established Communism anywhere outside Russia.

It was natural that the revolutionary order which the Russian Communists were proceeding to establish should provoke resistance, not only from other Russians who belonged to, or supported, the former propertied classes, but also from their sympathizers in other countries. The sudden murder of the Tsar and his family on the orders of the local soviet holding sway over the district to which the Royal Family had retired (an action afterwards approved by the Central Soviet), and the similar ruthless treatment dealt out to other members of the old regime, the exaltation of the manual workers who were put in responsible positions—all this spread alarm in Europe and beyond the Atlantic. Still more important was the fact that the Bolsheviks had made a separate peace with Germany. Civil war and war of intervention followed, and they were accompanied by famine and terrorism. To the outside world the next few years seemed full of confusion and misery, and many thought it was only a matter of time before the Communist Government would collapse. Lenin, however, never lost his way through the cloud of troubles that encompassed his regime. Some say of him that, unlike other great leaders, he did not try to impose his will on history but co-operated with the natural processes of historical development. Others say that he was the supreme opportunist. However it may be expressed, it is certain that his success depended on his readiness to do whatever the psychological moment required, and in this Stalin has been like him. Thus the peasants were allowed at first to give expression to their land hunger and occupy the old manorial estates, although later they were to be compelled to merge their holdings into large collective farms. Thus in 1921, after three years of triumph over the abolition of private property, private property and private trading were temporarily reinstalled in order to increase the supply of consumption goods—the N.E.P. policy (described on p. 62). Thus, when the world revolution failed to materialize, the policy of promoting world revolution was allowed to fall into the background, and one of national development superseded it. This last was a decision of the greatest importance. Once it was taken the flood of revolution was diverted into a channel, and no longer threatened to engulf the world. The Soviet Government began to lose some of the hostility and distrust with which other governments naturally regarded it, and to tread a path of foreign policy that eventually led to membership of the League of Nations. It should not be forgotten that Lenin accepted the momentous change of policy before his death, although the task of fulfilment was the responsibility of Stalin.

STALIN AND TROTSKY

The redirection of revolutionary energy was not carried out easily and peaceably. It involved, in the first place, a break with Trotsky. This dramatic figure was the chief orator of the Revolution, and although Communists are supposed not to be swayed by personal feelings there can be no doubt that outside the Party Trotsky had a personal hold on thousands who had been affected by his personality and his eloquence, while in the Party itself there were many who were convinced that he was right to denounce the betrayal of world revolution. It may be easily understood that Trotsky's contention that a Socialist State could never be built in Russia until revolution had been fomented in every other country, and the new and more modest proposal of Stalin to industrialize the Soviet Union on Socialist lines, constituted two very different appeals. The first policy was a call to the romantic revolutionary, the second to the practical administrator and patriot. The rival views of two leaders who were not only politically opposed, but also personally antagonistic, were hotly debated for two years in meetings of the Communist Party up and down the country until Trotsky's point of view was overwhelmingly defeated. This should have been an end of the matter, for Communist discipline demands that when a decision has been reached after due debate it must be loyally accepted. Trotsky, however, refused to accept the decision and threw all the dynamic force of his personality into a campaign against the decision. There gathered round him not only his personal adherents and honest supporters but all manner of dissatisfied people who saw in his resistance an opportunity to oppose Socialism and the Soviet Government. All kinds of sabotage, some of it perhaps imaginary, but much of it beyond question, began to threaten the success of the new industrial enterprises and to undermine the regime. The Government set out to exterminate all opposition. Up and down the Soviet Union, in engineering shops and railway undertakings, among school teachers, doctors, peasants, and soldiers, there was a ruthless search for any one with Trotsky-ite leanings. Hence there came about the series of purges which to the outer world seemed like another civil war but which in true Communist circles were regarded as no more than the necessary motions of a surgeon's knife removing a malignant growth. Some of the enemies of the regime were dispatched quietly, others were given public trials on the stages of theatres and before packed audiences. The intention was to demonstrate to the people how the counter-revolu-tionaries worked, how they were willing to connive at help from foreign enemies, how they would wreck machinery with deliberate sabotage, and how those who were well versed in Communist doctrine could be, through the force of argu-ment, persuaded of their wrong thinking and moved to con-fess their treachery. It was part of the policy of the Commun-ist leaders to make the whole country conscious of the dan-gers of disunity, but it was inevitable that the policy should also create fear at home and shocked incredulity in Britain and America, where the dramatic trials, the mass arrests, and the high-pitched articles in the Soviet press seemed to the Anglo-Saxon temperament to be a kind of amazing political hysteria.

The purges continued in a series of waves, and if they re-moved many who in other countries would have been accept-ed as honest critics, they also removed those to whom later events gave the name of quislings. This, in the light of future developments, was the justification for the removal of thou-sands of officers in the Red Army purge that came in 1937—

many years after the foundations of the Socialist industrial State had been well laid, and when the political organization of the country had been established. The security for the political and economic Socialist order built in Russia under Stalin's leadership was to depend ultimately on the strength and integrity of the Red Forces.

THE RED ARMY

The Red Army began as a revolutionary army in two senses. It was the fighting force of the revolutionary regime introduced by the Bolsheviks; but it was also, in its initial stage, a new army, organized in a new way.

The old Imperial army, with its several millions of soldiers, had rendered splendid service to the allied cause in the years 1914-1917, and this despite inadequate equipment, uncertain food supplies, and a growing disaffection in the ranks. Impaired as it was, it inflicted a disastrous defeat on the Austro-German forces in the summer of 1916. Nevertheless, by the spring of the next year, when the first revolution had taken place, it had mostly lost heart for the war.

The Bolsheviks appear to have been the only political party that realized the necessity of trying to win the support of the soldiers, and it was part of their policy during the six months between the first and second revolutions to increase their propaganda in the army and to encourage the formation of soldiers' committees. They published a soldiers' newspaper (*Soldiers' Truth*) and opened clubs for servicemen. At the same time they formed from the industrial workers a new proletarian militia, the Red Guards. These recruits, who were, in a sense, the fathers of the future Red Army, numbered about 10,000 by the time the Bolsheviks came to power.

Although it had been part of the Bolsheviks' propaganda to

promise a speedy end to the war, it had not been their intention to abolish the fighting forces of their country. They worked to re-create them according to revolutionary principles, on a basis of voluntary service, with officers elected by the ranks, and in a spirit of comradeship and equality. These ideas, although applied in the first flush of revolutionary success, had very soon to be abandoned.

The Imperial army's reaction to the Bolshevik revolution was to ask to go home or to go home without asking. The promise of peace, along with the two other promises of "bread" and "land", meant more to most soldiers, posted hundreds of miles from their own village, than political doctrine. Only certain units of the old Imperial forces—and these included some naval men spoiling for a fight—were ready to become the defenders of the new regime. Nevertheless, these, together with the Red Guards, would have sufficed for the time being had the Bolsheviks been only confronted with enemies at home. On February 1, 1918, however, the Germans broke off the peace negotiations, which it had been one of the first acts of the Bolsheviks to initiate, and a serious crisis developed.

It was necessary to raise immediately a new army to bar the way to the approaching Germans. On February 21 the Council of People's Commissars addressed the Russian people in a manifesto which began with the words: "Our socialist fatherland is in danger!" There was an immediate response from Petrograd, Moscow and other large towns, and in the meantime, on February 23, the first Red Army units sent to the front inflicted a defeat on the Germans near Pskov and Narva. This day has since been observed as the anniversary of the Red Army.

In March the unequal struggle with the Germans came to

an end with the Treaty of Brest Litovsk, and a breathing space followed in which the foundations of the new army of "workers and peasants" were laid. Conscription was introduced, local military commissariats were established for registering all men fit for service, and the following solemn pledge for all recruits was drawn up: "I promise that at the first call of the Workers' and Peasants' Government I will take up arms to defend the Soviet republic from all dangers and from all attacks of its enemies and that in the struggle for the Russian Soviet Republic, for the cause of Socialism, and the brotherhood of nations I will not spare my efforts or my life."

At the same time the system of military or political commissars was introduced. The responsibility of these men was to teach the soldiers the political creed of the new Russia and to act as security officers. Although the Red Army Commanders (i.e. officers) were solely responsible for military decisions, they fulfilled their duties under the watchful eyes of the commissars, and military orders had to be endorsed with the commissar's signature. This was a safeguard against secret counter-revolutionary tactics on the part of the commanders, many of whom had formerly served under the Tsar.

Despite Brest Litovsk, the Germans invaded the Ukraine, and at the same time Allied armies of intervention came to the aid of the "White" Russians who wished to restore the old regime. Civil war lasted until 1920 and at one time three quarters of Russian territory was in the hands of the enemies of the Bolsheviks. It was during this period that some of the leaders of the Red Army of to-day had their first experience of battle.

In the next twenty years little was known about the Red Army among the ordinary people of other countries, and in military circles there was a good deal of controversy as to what was its real strength. When it was revealed that a great number of officers had been liquidated in the purge of 1937 scepticism increased.

The opening phases of the Russo-Finnish war in the winter of 1939-1940 did nothing to correct the general view, for there was reliable evidence that the first Russian soldiers who were taken prisoner in Finland were inadequately clothed and ill-equipped, and it was some time before the numerical superiority of the Russians, and the better quality troops which they later sent to the front, gave them an advantage. Whether the Russians were not yet ready for war, or whether they were purposely hiding their strength are questions that the future may answer, but it is well known that when Russia was suddenly attacked by Germany in June 1941, the general opinion was that the Red Army would succumb. Since that date the real picture has emerged; the organization, strength and highly skilled leadership of the Soviet Forces, as well as the high standard of its equipment, are now common knowledge. It is not necessary to enlarge on this, and it is outside the purpose of this booklet to give any account of the strategy and campaigns which, after three years of most bitter warfare, brought the Red Army back through territories which had had to be temporarily abandoned to the enemy, to the capital of Germany itself.

The war, however, brought changes to some features of the Red Army and drew attention to others that were there before. Of these something must be said.

The dual control of commanders and political commissars had been abolished in 1940, but after the German attack in June 1941 the commissars were re-instated with newly defined functions. Their responsibility was now a two-fold one of morale and welfare and the political function faded into the background. What was expected of the commissars cannot be better expressed than in the words of Stalin at the time: "If the commander is the head of the regiment, the regiment's commissar must be its father and soul." He was to be "the moral leader of his unit, the first defender of its material and spiritual interests." In the opinion of a foreign observer: "the system keeps officers, as well as men, on their toes."

During the next fifteen months, from July 1941 until October 1942, the commissars went through the ordeal of battle with commanders and private soldiers. Those of higher rank —and they were graded like other soldiers—participated in important strategic and tactical decisions, and had thus become a natural reserve from which new military leaders could be drawn. In October 1942 the dual control of commissars and commanders was finally abolished, and all commissars who were considered suitable were given a special technical course at officers' training schools. Thence they returned to the army as both qualified and seasoned commanders. Those who were not suitable for this transfer continued their former work for the morale and welfare of the troops.

The status of the Russian officer became increasingly important during the recent war. Although at first Red Army commanders on leave in Moscow would appear in battledress and wearing their felt boots, this was later forbidden and best uniforms had to be worn. These uniforms, with their huge shoulder epaulettes, call to mind those of the old Russian army and are equally impressive. Although promotion to officer rank is open to all, the commanders are, by training as well as by the prestige which they enjoy, a highly honoured class in Soviet society. Their pay is commensurate with this;

a subaltern, for instance, receives more than five times the pay of a private soldier.

Men who become officers in the Red Army embark on a military career as a profession, and their status is likely to be enhanced in the future by the nine "Suvorov Schools" which were announced in August 1943 as part of a plan for post-war reconstruction. These are military training schools to which entrants normally go at the age of eight and stay till they are seventeen. Special places are reserved for the sons of Red Army officers who lost their lives in the war.

Education of a general nature and for civilian trades is a special feature of Red Army life in peace-time, and a man's period of conscript service has been an opportunity for many to learn to read and write, if they were illiterate, and also to learn a useful trade or pursue a hobby. There is also political instruction, and this still continues during active service. It consists partly of reading aloud from Moscow papers, and is designed to enable the Red Army man to understand both the cause for which he is fighting and to be aware of his Soviet citizenship.

Before the war the Red Army man, returning to his village after his period of service, played an important part as a champion of the regime, and was a useful link between his own people and the State. Returning from active service he has inevitably been regarded—and quite rightly—as a person of great consequence. Moreover, his heroism is enhanced by the fact that for all the skill and swift development which the Red Army represents, the Soviet soldiers have lacked the amenities which their British, and more particularly their American Allies, have been able to bring into the field.

III

HOW THE U.S.S.R. IS GOVERNED

WHILE the purges were clearing the new Russia of counter-revolutionaries and the outside world was bewildered by the trials and "liquidations," the process of constructing the Socialist State went steadily forward. In the next chapter we shall show how industry was built up on Socialist principles and collective farming introduced. While this immense effort of economic reconstruction was going forward, the political structure, the machinery of government and administration, was also being developed. It is this which we must now consider.

One of the surprising things about the Soviet State is that there was no preconceived programme for the Bolsheviks to follow after their revolutionary triumph. It might have been thought that Lenin, the intellectual and theorist, reading and writing for so many long years in his lodgings in Geneva and London, would have had some cut-and-dried scheme ready to apply to Russia after his victory. Marx, however, had never concerned himself with reconstruction but only with revolution, and Lenin had concentrated on the technique of making the revolt of the workers effective wherever it might happen. Always, as we have seen, Lenin developed his strategy according to the requirements immediately ahead.

The idea of a *Soviet* State, therefore, was not an idea that was conceived in theory and afterwards applied, but an idea that grew out of events. When soviets of workers and of soldiers sprang up spontaneously in Russia after the collapse of

Tsardom, Lenin saw that here were stepping-stones towards a second and a Bolshevik revolution. When later this revolution succeeded through the conversion of the soviets to Bolshevik ideas, the soviets became rocks on which to build. From different parts of the country the local soviets sent delegates to attend the Soviet Congress that met from time to time in the capital. At these meetings of revolutionary leaders and workpeople the Commissars (or Ministers) were elected and immediate policies agreed upon. Russia was to be henceforth a Soviet State. In the ensuing struggle with counter-revolutionaries the soviets could not exercise the democratic control over the Government that seemed at first to be their function and the Communist leaders in Moscow became more and more authoritarian. Nevertheless, the soviets remained ostensibly the machinery of government and this machinery was gradually developed and improved.

THE STALIN CONSTITUTION

For the first nineteen years the soviet system formed a pyramid of meetings and committees. At the base were all the factory and the village meetings which elected their representatives to the soviets of the factory and village. From these bodies delegates were sent to town and district soviets and so on up to the All-Union Soviet Congress. This was the general framework, but as time went on it grew in complexity and eventually it was replaced by a system of parliamentary and local government based on elected representatives chosen from particular geographical areas. This system was embodied in a written Constitution offered in 1936 to the peoples of the U.S.S.R. for their comment, and adopted with a few emendations at the end of that year. It is said to be very largely the personal work of Stalin and is often spoken of as the Stalin

Constitution. As the U.S.S.R. is a socialist State, the Constitution deals inevitably with the ownership and organization of industry as well as with political machinery. In the following description of the Constitution we shall, as far as possible, disregard the industrial organization, although the industrial and political systems of the U.S.S.R. are necessarily interlocked. The articles of the Constitution dealing with the economic and industrial framework will be described in the next chapter.

Each of the sixteen Union Republics that together form the U.S.S.R. is in certain respects self-governing, but all are linked together in the All-Union parliament which meets in Moscow every six months and more often if necessary. This parliament consists of two Chambers: one of these, the *Soviet of the Union*, is elected on the same principle as the British House of Commons—that is to say, each member represents a certain geographical district, or constituency, and is elected by the adult population of that district. In view of the vastness of Russia, however, every member has to represent a far larger number of constituents than does the British M.P. In Britain we think 80,000 a large number to be represented by one member of the House of Commons, but in the U.S.S.R. each representative stands for 300,000 of his fellow countrymen.

The Second Chamber of the Soviet Union, the *Soviet of the Nationalities*, has no parallel in our own country, but in its composition it may be compared with the Senate in the U.S.A., for both are especially constituted to give equal representation to all the States in the Union. In the Soviet of the Nationalities there are twenty-five representatives from each Republic of the Union, regardless of its size and importance. Thus the Russian Soviet Federated Socialist Republic or the R.S.F.S.R. (by far the largest of the Republics), in

D

spite of its population of 100 millions, is no more strongly represented than Tadzhikistan with its one and a half millions.

Besides the representation for each self-governing State, other groups of people in defined areas within the various States can also elect representatives to the Second Chamber. Such areas are called "Autonomous Republics," "Autonomous Regions," and "National Areas," and, although not raised to the position of a Union Republic, they have a measure of self-government. Autonomous Republics send eleven deputies to the Soviet of Nationalities, Autonomous Regions, five, and National Areas, one.

Since the word Soviet is embedded in the history of revolutionary Russia, it is natural that it should be applied to the two Houses of the Russian parliament. The parliament, as a whole, is called the *Supreme Soviet*. (It should be noted that in some earlier English references to the U.S.S.R. Constitution the word Council is used in place of Soviet.)

In a general way the work of the Supreme Soviet may seem similar to that of any other parliament—laws are made, the budget is agreed on, policies are discussed and the work of government departments (commissariats) is criticized. The usual procedure for the introduction of a new Bill is as follows. The responsible commissar introduces the Bill to a full meeting of the Supreme Soviet. The parliament then adjourns while a special commission of members considers the Bill in detail. This draws up a report on the Bill, proposing various amendments and making criticisms, and the report is later given to the re-assembled parliament. A general debate follows and the commissar makes a concluding speech in which he accepts such amendments as he considers reasonable. The debate on the 1940 Budget provides some illustrations of this. When the special commission of members had considered the financial proposals of the Commissar of Finance—whose position is comparable to that of our Chancellor of Exchequer —a woman member in presenting the report to the full parliament stated, among other items of criticism and amendment, that her commission proposed an increase in revenue of over a thousand million roubles, and explained how the money could be raised. She also reported that her commission found fault with the way in which certain Government departments were carrying out their work, in particular the Commissariats of Machine Industry and of Building Materials. She called to task the Commissariat of Finance (corresponding to our Treasury) for not exercising a sterner control over the manner in which these departments spent public money. She further asked for a greater sum of money to be allocated to Ukraine to cover a shortage of working capital in that Republic. In the debate which followed a representative of the small Asiatic Republic of Uzbekistan asked for money to be allocated for a new railway, and a Moscow representative demanded more grants for culture and educational developments in the capital. Later a member from Azerbaijan complained that the budget did not allocate the necessary money for further developing the oilfields in his Republic. In winding up the debate the Commissar of Finance accepted most of the suggestions, including the initial and important one for increasing the revenue. The Budget, in its amended form, was then passed clause by clause.

In some respects this debate calls to mind a Budget debate in the British parliament, but any such comparison is apt to be superficial and overlooks significant differences. First and foremost, it is important to remember that there is only one party in the Supreme Soviet, and although a proportion of the elected representatives may not be Party members they are inevitably in general agreement with Party policy, for no political opposition, as we understand the word, is allowed in the U.S.S.R. An examination of the proceedings of any sitting of the Supreme Soviet is likely to reveal outspoken criticism on the management of affairs and on points of detail. But contrasted, for example, with the uncompromising judgement pronounced by some British M.P.s on Mr Chamberlain's policy of appeasement, with the sweeping denunciation of the British economic system sometimes delivered by the left-wing members of the British parliament, or with the forcible objections originally brought to bear by isolationist American Senators on Mr Roosevelt's lease-lend proposals, the difference becomes clear. The expressions of pride and pleasure in the Soviet system with which most Russian representatives begin their speeches emphasize the underlying uniformity which binds them.

There are other differences also which are worth noting. There is, for instance, in the Russian parliament a permanent nucleus of members, the *Presidium*, elected by the rest to carry on the work between the sessions. Decisions of the Presidium have to be approved by the full parliament, but this body nevertheless seems to hold a position superior to that of the full parliament. It can call for the dissolution of the Supreme Soviet and it elects the People's Commissars. These are the heads of the Government departments and correspond to Ministers of State in other countries.

Another and a very interesting feature of the Supreme Soviet is the close relationship maintained between every member and his constituency. Every member is expected to report to the Supreme Soviet on local conditions, and on his return to his constituency he must give the electors an account of the proceedings in parliament. This relationship holds good for local soviets also, and in every case a member who does not seem to be carrying out his political functions satisfactorily may be "recalled" by his constituents and replaced by another representative. As it is usual at election time for substitutes to be elected along with the actual members, and as these have the right of attending all soviet meetings as observers, it may be presumed that an unsatisfactory representative can easily be replaced.

The procedure in the Supreme Soviet is reproduced in the parliament of each Union republic. These parliaments are known as the Supreme Soviets of the particular republic which they cover but only consist of one House. They have their own Presidium and these appoint such Commissars as are required for State affairs as distinct from all-Union matters. For example, each State has among others its Commissariats for Health and Education. Until recently Defence and Foreign Affairs were All-Union responsibilities, but under a decree published in February 1944 the separate Republics were given the right to have their own departments for Foreign Affairs and Defence. As a result of this, the constituent Republics may raise their own armies and have their own diplomatic representatives in other countries.

The local government of town and village in Russia is roughly on the same lines as local government elsewhere, but there is one striking and interesting difference. In other countries the work that is carried out under the direction of local authorities is undertaken entirely by paid employees— medical officers, sanitary inspectors, school attendance officers and so on. In the U.S.S.R. much of this work is performed by the members of the councils themselves. Every elected person is appointed to some section of local government work and expected to give some of his time to it, either leisure time or work time or both. Whether this arrangement makes for inefficiency it is impossible to say, but it certainly means that men and women who serve on local soviets have an intimate knowledge of the needs of their localities, and it must assuredly result in enthusiastic and energetic persons being elected. But here again, the elected members must be either Communists or supporters of Communist policy.

To complete this sketch of the Soviet Government's machine, something must be said about voters. In the U.S.S.R. every man and woman has the right to vote for every kind of soviet from the age of eighteen, unless he is mentally deficient or has been deprived of his right by a court of law. Candidates must, however, have reached the age of twenty-three. It is usual for groups of citizens to put forward nominations. For instance, a collective farm or a factory will have its favourite candidates who will be nominated by all the workers meeting together in their place of work. Their proposals will be put forward at a special local conference representing all the nominating bodies convened some time before the elections, and by a gradual process of discussion and elimination the number of candidates will be reduced, very frequently to one only. Thus, although on election day itself the voters may only be asked to come and give their assent by secret ballot to certain already selected persons, these final nominees have in fact been chosen as the result of prolonged and open argument. No election is valid unless at least 50 per cent of the voters have polled, and in a contested election the candidate, to be successful, must have an absolute majority over his opponents. Although party politics are absent from soviet elections, the day when votes are recorded is full of excitement. The Communist Party considers it a matter of great importance that every citizen should exercise his right, for one of the principles of communism is that there should be the widest possible interest and participation in public affairs. Accordingly, posters and banners hang across the streets urging every one to go and vote.

When one considers how many are the occasions on which the modern citizen of the U.S.S.R. is called upon to vote, it is impossible not to feel that he and she must be getting all the political education that the makers of the new Russia could desire. Consider, for example, the voting opportunities of a modern citizen of the Crimea, which is in the R.S.F.S.R., but constitutes an "Autonomous Republic." First, as a citizen of the whole U.S.S.R. he must vote for his representative in the Soviet of the Union (which we compared with our own House of Commons) and also for the 25 representatives of his own State (i.e. the R.S.F.S.R.) in the Soviet of Nationalities. But since he lives in an "Autonomous Republic" he must also choose five representatives from the Crimea to sit in the Soviet of Nationalities. These are all elections to the U.S.S.R. Supreme Soviet. There will be another election for his own State parliament, the Supreme Soviet of the R.S.F.S.R., and there still remain the purely local elections. Supposing the citizen we have in mind lives in Sevastopol, he will take part in the election of the Sevastopol city soviet; on the other hand, if he lives in a village there will be two local elections, one for his village soviet and one for his district soviet.

Even this is not the full story of the citizen's political life. If he works in a factory he will be encouraged to belong to a trade union and take part in the elections of a factory trade union committee. If, on the other hand, he is a peasant working on a collective farm he must vote for the committee that supervises the farm organization. In a country where all factories and farms are publicly owned such elections at a man's place of work are, in a sense, political. In the course of election meetings for trade union or farm committee a worker may have complaints that he wishes to voice—for example, a plea for better housing or for irrigation developments. Such complaints have to be passed on by the elected representatives to the appropriate soviet.

So far we have given a short description of the machinery of government in the U.S.S.R. and most of what has been said may be found in the 1936 Constitution. But only incidentally in the Constitution do we find reference to the power which works this machinery. Without the driving force of the Communist Party the elaborate structure would become meaningless and ineffectual. It is interesting to notice that at the time when Stalin produced his Constitution he himself held no position of official importance. He was not then a People's Commissar, and held no more important office in the political organization than that of an elected member of parliament. But as General Secretary of the Communist Party of the Soviet Union he held the key position of Party leader and, more than any other, was responsible for the life and success of the Soviet regime.

THE COMMUNIST PARTY

The Communist Party in Russia has remained essentially what Lenin made it. It is still as it was in the beginning, a party that no one can join easily, and from which unsatisfactory members are immediately expelled. There is no other party or organization with which it can be fairly compared. Like soldiers in their regard to discipline, like missionaries in their sense of vocation, Russian Communists are, nevertheless, more self-responsible than the ordinary soldier and without the missionary's sense of divine support. New recruits are chiefly from younger men and women, and many of them have already had a preliminary training in the Communist Youth Movement (Komsomol) and before that in the Pioneers, a juvenile organization. To these younger citizens Party membership has much to offer, and the hardships are no deterrent. They cheerfully plunge into a kind of guerrilla warfare against anything that might weaken the regime, whatever it may be. In their work they must set an example by being more industrious than others; in both work and leisure they must be alert to explain the policy of the Government to any one who grumbles or criticizes; they must not drink immoderately or waste their time; they are expected to keep their income to a moderate level by contributing any surplus to Party funds; they must not belong to any church or to any other society that would divide their allegiance; when travelling by boat or train they must make themselves known to transport officials and be ready to help them; but, most particularly, they must take an active part in the political system, coming to the fore at all meetings and getting themselves or other suitable candidates elected on to committees and to posts of responsibility. To maintain the highest possible level of Party behaviour the members submit themselves to periodic tests. On these occasions they appear on a platform and confront not only their fellow members, but also their fellow workers or neighbours, and give an account of themselves. Remorseless criticism follows, the chairman begging the audience not to waste time in giving praise, but to produce any evidence of failure, slackness, or other counter-revolutionary behaviour. At the end a number of members find themselves either dismissed or suspended. Dismissal may come from above also, for at the Politbureau, the "Cabinet" of the Party in Moscow, a register of all members is kept and is revised from time to time. If when a change of policy occurs some members do not accept the new Party "line," they will of course have to leave the Party. As has already been stated, discussion is invited before the new line is adopted; once, however, the decision is taken every member must actively support it, even if what he is now asked to proclaim seems to contradict the pronouncements of a short while ago.

The Party is organized on a nation-wide basis behind the political machine; it is, in fact, the power behind the machine. In any factory or other industrial undertaking the Party members will form a group, formerly called a cell, but later described as a primary organ. If they are sufficiently numerous they will elect their factory Communist committee which will watch over the output of the factory and the morale of the workers. (This, of course, is quite distinct from the trade union committee which, as already mentioned, is responsible for the welfare of the worker.) City and district conferences of the Party are attended by delegates from these primary groups, who elect their local committee. The Central Committee of the Party is elected by ballot at the All-Union Party Congress. As in the factories, so in the villages, although here the proportion of the Communists to the non-party citizens is usually smaller than in the industrial centres, and occasionally a lone Communist will bear on his or her shoulders the full responsibility of making his neighbours well disposed towards the government and the regime. Yet again, each country district will have its Communist Committee, forming part of the Party pyramid, which has its base over the whole of the U.S.S.R. and its apex in Moscow.

During the time of the Revolution and for some years afterwards the few thousand Communists who then composed the

Party had to be sent all over the country visiting town and village to explain the basis of the new Socialist State, the changes that must take place, and the future classless, democratic and prosperous country that all good Communists believed would one day reward their efforts. These missionaries sowed their seed well, and gradually there developed from end to end of the Union what may be described as native Communist groups. This was what was desired. Soon after the Bolshevik revolution the former Tsarist dependencies had been declared self-governing republics, with a right to break away from the mother country. All the same, the intention was to bind them by strong Party links so that they would not wish to secede. It must be reckoned as one of the Party's great achievements that the Union has held together and that a kind of invisible grid carries the power of the regime from Moscow to Ukraine, Uzbekistan, and even the Soviet Far East.

The Communist Party is still a small Party, numbering perhaps about two and a half million out of the whole population, and although membership was made easier during the war years the policy seems to be to restrict the members to something like this limit. It should not be assumed, however, that all these Party members, or even the majority of them, have been elected to the various soviets. They have no outward and obvious monopoly of the Party machine. When a local Communist group attends, for instance, a village meeting at which nominations for the village soviet are to be made, it certainly has a list of men and women whom it wishes to propose, but the list will only include a proportion of Party members, and even these will not necessarily all be elected. The Russian peasants are a stubborn, cautious and reflective people, not to be won over by fine-sounding words.

To the foreign visitor before the war the Party member's tirelessness in argument was something which left a strong, and, it must be admitted, often irritating impression. Well trained in Communist doctrines, his mind packed with statistics, blandly ignorant and rather contemptuous of conditions in other countries, the Party man or woman was ready at any hour of the day or night to instruct compatriot or foreigner alike. He was never nonplussed and rarely ruffled. His convictions were like granite, his outlook materialistic. Despising religion, yet speaking as if with religious conviction, his whole being was merged in the creation of a new social order. It was not difficult for the easy-going citizen from another kind of society to see his limitations. On the other hand, it is he who has made the new Russia, and it is because of his limitations that he has succeeded. He is the product of a revolution which felt the world to be in arms against it. A more peaceable world and a prosperous and, above all, a secure Russia might well produce a new kind of Communist.

The last word has not been said on the Soviet political machine until mention has been made of the Secret Police, formerly known as the O.G.P.U.[1] Although since 1934 it has not been an independent organization but part of the Commissariat for Internal Affairs (the N.K.V.D.) it seemed to operate much as before up to the time of the war. Partly a public police organization concerned with such matters as passports and ordinary public safety, it was, nevertheless, chiefly known in its more sinister aspect as a vast body of secret agents whose task was to round up, try, and execute counter-revolutionaries. One of the most painstaking, and at the same time most sympathetic, of investigations into the

[1] The translation of the title for which these letters stand is "Union State Political Administration." The O.G.P.U. superseded a similar organization, the Cheka, in 1922.

U.S.S.R., while showing that the O.G.P.U. is the direct descendant of the Tsarist Secret Police, nevertheless condemned it unreservedly: "There is something ghastly in its inveterate secretiveness, even down to the detail of making nearly all its arrests in the dead of night. The public hears nothing until a brief notice in the newspapers informs it that a sentence has been carried out."[1] This however relates to some years ago, and conditions change rapidly in the Soviet Union.

[1] Sidney and Beatrice Webb, *Soviet Communism.*

IV

THE STRUGGLE FOR PROSPERITY & SECURITY

THE SOCIALIST STATE

"THE Union of Soviet Socialist Republics," runs the first Article of the U.S.S.R. Constitution, "is a socialist State of workers and peasants," and the next eleven Articles give substance to this declaration.

"The economic foundation of the U.S.S.R.," says Article Four, "is the socialist system of economy and the socialist ownership of the implements of production firmly established as a result of the liquidation of the capitalist system of economy, the abolition of private property in the implements and means of production, and the abolition of exploitation of man by man." Articles Five to Eight explain the ways in which property may be owned in the U.S.S.R. Most sources of wealth—for example, land and forests, factories, mills and mines, railways and waterways—are the property of the State, "that is, the possession of the whole people." In the case of the collective farms, however, all the produce, livestock, farm buildings, and farm implements are in the possession of each farming community, and the farm land, although the property of the State, is secured to the peasant groups, "for their free use for an unlimited time, that is, for ever."

Articles Nine and Ten answer questions that have often been asked by people outside the U.S.S.R.: Can no one in the U.S.S.R. do business on his own account? And are there no private personal possessions?

Article Nine.—"Alongside the socialist system of economy, which is the predominant form of economy in the U.S.S.R., the law permits small private economy of individual peasants and handicrafts based on their personal labour and precluding the exploitation of the labour of others."

Article Ten.—"The right of citizens to personal property in their income from work and in their savings, in their dwelling houses and auxiliary household economy, their domestic furniture and utensils and objects of personal use and comfort, as well as the right of inheritance of personal property of citizens, are protected by law."

Article Eleven explains that "the economic life of the U.S.S.R. is determined and directed by the State plan of national economy," which aims at increasing the wealth of the nation, and steadily raising both the material and cultural level of the people, making the U.S.S.R. independent and strengthening its power of defence. But all citizens are expected to share in the general responsibility, as Article 12 makes clear:

"In the U.S.S.R. work is the obligation and a matter of honour of every able-bodied citizen, in accordance with the principle: 'He who does not work, neither shall he eat.'

"In the U.S.S.R. the principle of socialism is realized: 'From each according to his ability, to each according to the work performed.' "

The last maxim shows that there are no pretensions about equality of income in the Russian Socialist State. It perhaps also raises the question as to whether the Communists are right in their claim to be establishing a "classless society." From the Communists' point of view there is no contradiction, for in Communist doctrine a classless society does not mean a society where there are no social grades or diversity of incomes, but one in which there are no landlords, capitalists, and employers on the one hand, and dependent wage-earners on the other.

It is not surprising that the Soviet Constitution should open with these ringing pronouncements on the Socialist State. As we have seen, the abolition of capitalism in favour of a socialist economy was the real purpose of the Communist Revolution. Its success and survival in one country, despite the misgivings and scepticism of the surrounding capitalist[1] world, was a success that could not be viewed by those who made it without some challenging satisfaction. Nor can there be any question that these Articles of the Constitution represent the actual conditions in the country. The economic order established in Russia is socialist and therefore fundamentally different from that which has hitherto prevailed in all other countries. Under the capitalist system material progress has come as the result of the profit motive. What was to be provided, how much of it and when, depended on the separate decisions of individual business men, and they were guided in their decisions by their desire for profit. This was the economic system of Russia before the Revolution, and it is the system which has prevailed in the rest of the world, even in Germany and Italy, where Fascism went far in imposing state control on business enterprise. The Russian Revolution broke the mainspring of capitalist economics and put in its place the national economic Plan. The State Planning Authority, Gosplan, guided by the Council of Commissars and the Communist Party, determines what factories should be

---

[1] The word capitalist is used here not in any political sense, but as a technical term denoting an economic system in which the means of production are privately owned, and in which the profit motive determines the allocation of the resources of production.

built, what new mines sunk, what new oil wells bored, what
shops, cinemas, and offices established.

Again, under the capitalist system, the means of production
—the land, mines, factories, and so on—have been, with certain exceptions, in private hands. In Soviet Russia, however,
the means of production are not privately owned, and there
are no such things as commercial companies and sharehold-
ers. Certain small one-man businesses are still allowed, but
apart from these there is public ownership of all industries
and all public services.

FROM THE REVOLUTION TO N.E.P.

The present economic order in Russia was not built in a
day, and was preceded by chaos and emergency measures.
Just as the Bolshevik revolutionaries had no cut-and-dried
scheme of political government prepared against the day of
their success, so they were unprepared with a clean-cut
system for dealing with production. The immediate result of
the revolution, as we have seen, was the seizure of the factories by the workers, but however much psychological satisfaction this reversal of power may have brought, it could not
guarantee the supply of goods—still less of weapons of war.
The most zealous band of factory workers do but waste their
time if they continue to make something which is not wanted.
This the revolutionary leaders fully understood, and a few
weeks after the Bolshevik success the first planning authority
met in the capital—a small conference of trade union leaders,
workers and technicians, who faced the stupendous task of
determining the needs of a nation that stretched from the
Gulf of Finland to Central Asia, and how these needs were to
be met. Even while the delegates talked, the German guns
were advancing in the west and counter-revolutionary forces

E

collecting in the south. A period of improvisation was inevitable. Factory committees were replaced by managers, and all industries nationalised. Many works closed down; others were urged to supply the needs of the Red Army; food was requisitioned from the peasants. The end of the civil war three years later found the country so hungry, impoverished and chaotic that private enterprise on a small scale and for certain industries was re-introduced as the speediest way to bring relief. This was known as the New Economic Policy or "N.E.P." The temporary abandonment of principles led the critics of the regime to conclude that the revolution had failed in its main purpose. Lenin, however, declared that he had taken one step backwards in order to take two forward. He wanted to stimulate the peasants into growing more grain with the bait of cheap purchases—calico, soap, tobacco and shoes, for instance—offered for sale by the N.E.P. men. His policy was successful and that it was indeed only a temporary measure became apparent when a few years later the N.E.P. men found themselves encompassed with difficulties. Deprived of the honour of voting for the soviets, heavily taxed, continually under suspicion as enemies of the regime, many of them sought more secure employment in State factories or went into compulsory or voluntary exile.

By 1928 the N.E.P. chapter was closed and the First Five-Year Plan was launched. This and the two plans which followed it have been much discussed outside Russia. They are generally thought of as a succession of industrial drives involving the building of new factories and plants at an ambitious rate. This, however, is only part of the picture, a snapshot, so to speak, of the most impressive gesture in a great national movement. It leaves out of view both the reason for the Plans and their enormous range.

THE FIVE-YEAR PLANS

We have seen that Stalin's successful struggle against Trotsky meant the end of romantic dreams of world revolution and the decision to concentrate on Russia's national security. The first Five-Year Plan was the first manifestation of Russia's new policy. On the basis of data collected by the State Planning Authority (Gosplan) during the years when the issue of the struggle between Stalin and Trotsky hung in the balance, the first programme of national progress was finally announced. But it was to be progress on all fronts; not only was there to be a speed-up of industrialization, but the eighty per cent of the people who were peasants were to be swept into collective farms. At the same time there was to be an intensified attack against illiteracy, a great building of schools, of workers' dwellings, of clubs, cinemas, theatres and hospitals. For all this a new national spirit was invoked from the people and an attempt made to replace the now liquidated profit-incentive by a new motive. In a thousand speeches the workers and peasants were reminded that the potential wealth of the country was their own possession and that the labour that they gave to extracting it could only benefit themselves. Nor were the Plans merely forced upon the people by the Gosplan experts; on the contrary, one of the most interesting features of the movement was the way in which the workers made their own proposals and counter-proposals. In all the chief factories it was the usual procedure for the workpeople to meet and discuss the particular assignment which had been proposed for them by Gosplan on the basis of information previously supplied. The assignment would be scrutinized and criticized and a process of proposal and counter-proposal would continue during the months preceding the final introduction of each Plan. Similar meetings occurred in schools, colleges and sports clubs and among local soviet members. Every locality and every institution in fact had its plan and if no plan was sent to it from Moscow, it sent to Moscow its own proposals. By so doing it not only became incorporated in the great national advance, but could hope to receive an allocation out of the special funds at the disposal of Gosplan. Thus, in the months before each new national Plan thousands of proposals poured into Gosplan from end to end of the Soviet Union, and requests ranged from well-substantiated arguments in favour of irrigation schemes to demands for equipment for kindergartens and chess boards for workers' clubs. Then, when the Plan was launched every attempt was made to keep the public plan-conscious. In the course of the first Five-Year Plan streamers waved across the streets bearing the slogan "The Five-Year Plan—in Four" (it was in fact accomplished in less than five years); bare walls and the sides of tramcars, where in other countries commercial advertisements would compete for attention, were plastered with similar appeals. Newspaper headlines, ignoring foreign events, announced the first economic victories.

The core of the Plans was nevertheless economic; everything depended on the national leaders being able to show that the socialist system was bringing prosperity and security. It is important therefore to look now at the Plans from this point of view, examining first of all the changes in industry, then the revolution in agriculture, and finally the progress achieved.

The original idea was that the first Five-Year Plan should be directed, on the industrial front, to the development of heavy industry. When this stage had been passed the country would have its machinery for the production of consumers' goods—clothing, boots and shoes, household utensils and so on—and with this end in view the workers were asked to forgo a higher standard of living for the time being. Like soldiers accepting hardships under the assurance of ultimate victory, the workers tackled the Five-Year Plan on short rations. There was, for instance, a rationing of bread and a shortage of grain, for grain was one of the items that had to be exported in order to acquire foreign currency. At the outset there were many raw materials and machine tools that had to be purchased abroad and also foreign technicians were needed; and the Soviet Government could not, at that time hope for foreign credits. It was obliged therefore to sell abroad in order to buy abroad.

Unhappily, although the Five-Year Plan was completed ahead of time, the international situation began to deteriorate just as the second Five-Year Plan, with its promise of a more comfortable life, was being prepared and launched. In 1931 Japan invaded Manchuria. In 1933 Hitler and the Nazi Party assumed power in Germany. The second Five-Year Plan had therefore to be revised in order to make increased provision for weapons of war, and although, in the course of it, bread rationing came to an end and various material benefits began to be felt, both by peasants and town dwellers, progress in this direction was slowed down and the promised prosperity receded.

The third Five-Year Plan, begun in 1937 and due to finish in 1942, was the most comprehensive of the three, but it chiefly pointed towards strengthening Russia against attack and to this end the new industries already installed in eastern Russia—in the Urals, Siberia, the Far East, and Soviet Central Asia—were to be further developed. Despite this emphasis on defence the successful launching of this third

national programme made the picture of a prosperous and
secure Russia seem to be not a vision but a practical possibility if only war did not intervene, or could, at least, be postponed. The foundations had already been laid; it was a race
against the oncoming storm.

NATURAL RESOURCES OF THE U.S.S.R.

The opportunities were immense. The U.S.S.R. is not
only the largest country in the world but possibly the richest.
Of all the important raw materials necessary to our industrial
civilization she lacks none but rubber. Even that deficiency
may be remedied if rubber-bearing plants such as that discovered in the sandy wastes of Turkmenistan prove to be
worth exploiting, or if the synthetic rubber industries can be
adequately developed. With some sources of material wealth
the U.S.S.R. is better supplied than any other country. The
belt of forest, 600 miles deep, that stretches right across the
country south of the tundra, contains a supply of timber that
is quite unrivalled. The water power of Russia's great rivers
is greater than that of any other system of national waterways. There are more minerals for fertilizing purposes, more
iron, more manganese and possibly more gold than in any
other country; and the reserves of oil under Russian soil are
estimated at a total which is equal to that of all the deposits
in other countries combined. The coal reserves of Russia are
second only to those of the United States. Nickel, essential
in armaments and formerly thought to be absent, has been
discovered in the tundra, and the deposits are said to rank the
U.S.S.R. second to Canada, the chief source of nickel supplies for the world. Copper, of which there was formerly supposed to be a deficiency, now proves to be in good supply,
and tin, also once regarded as very scarce, is now found in

Central Asia. Lead and zinc, bauxite and chrome ore are also in good supply. Moreover, as we have already seen, Russian territory contains some of the richest soil in the world, reaching from eastern Ukraine to the further shores of the Black Sea and beyond the Urals, while in the Caucasus and Central Asia are great fertile regions suitable for such sub-tropical crops as tea, tobacco, cotton and Mediterranean fruits. To these may be added the apparently limitless miles of grassland for pasture.

A country so richly supplied with minerals and able to produce its own food and clothing might have been expected to take a leading place in the industrial world before now. But under the Tsars the resources of the country remained for the most part either undiscovered or unexploited, except in so far as they were found in the west. The economic development of the country was therefore one-sided. The industrial areas were almost entirely limited to the regions of Leningrad, Moscow and Eastern Ukraine. Ukraine offered the easiest prospects of development since the two basic raw materials of industry, coal and iron, were found in close conjunction—coal near the banks of the Donetz (tributary of the Don), iron in the region of Krivoi Rog. Nevertheless, it cannot be said that in these earlier days industrial plants and factories were built with an eye on local raw material. The fuelling of the industries of Moscow and Leningrad, for instance, was not based on the nearby coalfields—producing brown coal which needed special treatment for coking purposes—or on the local peat, a source of fuelling entirely overlooked, but on coal supplies from the distant Donetz mines. Again, the cotton mills were not found in Russian Central Asia, where the cotton grows, but in the opposite (north-west) corner of the country.

The danger of this concentration of industry in Western Russia was only too apparent when the Germans advanced over the Russian plains, and it was fully recognized by the designers of the Five-Year Plans. Although the older industrial centres, far from being neglected, were made to increase their output, there was considerable re-orientation. A cotton mill near Leningrad, for instance, was taken to pieces and set up again in Uzbekistan. Moscow and Leningrad were made to depend more on local fuel. But much more important was the great drive to make the new industrial areas in the east of equal importance with the west. Their successful development was a matter of life and death for the Soviet Union, and the new industries had to serve a variety of needs. They had, for example, to provide the necessary armaments and equipment for Russia's eastern armies so that these forces, guarding the Pacific frontier, need not depend for their supplies on consignments travelling 6,000 miles along the Trans-Siberian railway. They had, again, to be a reserve of supplies for the armies of the west if these should have to retire and, in retreat, lose the arsenals that would normally supply them. But quite apart from the equipment of armies, and also of air force and navy—they had to supply civilian needs. Russian farming, as we shall see presently, has been mechanized; this means that the food supply depends on tractors, lorries, combines, and these again on oil. Nor could the need to increase the standard of living of the people be entirely set aside, however the war clouds might threaten, for how could the Soviet leaders hope that the one hundred and ninety-three millions would be proof against enemy propaganda or would have the heart to stand the strains and miseries of war, if the regime for which they were called upon to labour as yet offered none of those attractions so long promised? If the ordinary conveniences of domestic life were still lacking in parts of Western Russia, they were still more lacking to the east of the Volga. In the forests of Siberia there were hunters and trappers who saw an aeroplane before they had ever seen a motor-car, so cut off were they from the outer world; and in the round felt tents of the nomads of Central Asia even the paraffin lamp was unknown, and the only light was an improvised wick embedded in animal fat. Yet these were the people, together with the shepherds of the Urals and the fur-wrapped Samoyeds of the Arctic Circle, who had to be persuaded to work in the new mines, oilfields, power stations, mills and factories, and on the new collective farms and plantations.

It is difficult on the available information to show the full extent to which new industries in the less vulnerable and undeveloped parts of the U.S.S.R. have been set up under the Plans. The most that could be done would be to draw up a list that would be so long and so full of strange names that it could hardly conjure up the actual picture of what has been happening. It seems best, therefore, to select a few enterprises that had a special interest and connection with the war, and in particular those concerned with coal, iron, oil and gold.

COAL, IRON AND STEEL

First of all there is the Ural-Kuznetz Combine. The term combine has quite a different meaning in Russia from elsewhere; it signifies a large unit of Soviet enterprise including a number of industrial works. In this case two regions, each rich in its own minerals and over a thousand miles apart, have been worked as one great enterprise for the production of iron and steel. In the southern Urals is Magnitnaya, or "Magnet"

Mountain, with iron ore only a little below the surface. There were some iron mines here in pre-Revolution days, but the output was small, and the ore was carried away by horses to a small foundry sixty miles distant. It was one of the projects of the first Five-Year Plan to develop these mines in conjunction with the coalfields near Kuznetz away to the east. Kuznetz was at that time the chief township in a central region of Southern Siberia, near the Altai Mountains. Here, in a sparsely inhabited countryside that has a short vivid summer, when for four months crops and flowers are prolific, and a long ice-bound winter that comes suddenly in September, there was abundant coal. In the foothills of the Altai Mountains it could be seen in great seams. Soviet geologists have estimated that the total amount would be sufficient to supply the whole world for three hundred years.

The basis of the Ural-Kuznetz scheme was that the iron of Magnet Mountain and the coal of Kuznetz should be interchanged, the trucks, on a specially constructed railway, going one way loaded with coal and the other way loaded with iron, and that iron and steel works should be built at both termini. By the end of the first Five-Year Plan the scheme was a going concern and it has been increasingly developed. New mines and new foundries have been established, and various subsidiary undertakings, such as chemical works and the making of fireproof materials, have been brought into the combine. Dozens of blast furnaces now blaze in the Urals and, at the foot of the Magnet Mountains, the little village of Magnetaya has grown, like an industrial mushroom, into a city the size of Coventry with the new name of Magnitogorsk. Here are streets and squares and parks, train and bus services, a power station and waterworks, technical institutes, schools, hospitals, a theatre, cinemas, a stadium and a circus. At the other end of the industrial road a similar new city, Stalinsk, has been built four miles from Kuznetz.

One feature of the third Five-Year Plan was the development of a new coalfield to feed the Ural iron and steel works. This was at Karaganda, in Kazakhstan, which, as a glance at the map will show, is a good deal nearer the Southern Urals than Kuznetz. It was estimated that by 1942 half the coal supply of the Ural furnaces would come from here. This was clearly a great advantage, even though the Karaganda coal has to travel on the newly constructed railway for a distance equal to that from London to the north of Scotland. Unfortunately, although there is a plentiful supply of coal in the Ural Mountains, it is not suitable for coking purposes and can only be used to a limited extent in the Ural industries.

The industrial development of the Urals is by no means confined to the Black Country now created round Magnitogorsk. From this, the most southerly point in the range, right up to the frozen heights in the Arctic Circle, the hills and valleys are dotted about with factory chimneys, mine shafts, newly built armament works, aircraft factories and industrial towns. The whole range is rich in a variety of minerals, the most important after iron being copper. Four-fifths of Russia's copper comes from here and among the various centres of copper mining and smelting the town of Degtyerki is probably the chief.

OIL AND GOLD

Equally important with coal and iron is oil. Formerly the oilfields of the Caucasus—at Baku, Grozny, and Maikop—were the sole sources of supply for Russia. They still hold priority of place, but their situation in the southernmost point of the U.S.S.R. was obviously so inconvenient for peace-time supplies, and so vulnerable in war-time, that the Soviet Government have long been prospecting for new reserves. On the assumption that a great belt of oil-producing strata stretches northwards from the neighbourhood of the Caspian Sea, new wells have been bored and with the most satisfactory results. In the plain between the western slopes of the Urals and the River Volga oil is, in the words of the Soviet engineers, "gushing up" and the region is spoken of as "a second Baku." A chain of five new oil districts now runs from the Caspian to the Arctic—the first in the desert of western Turkmenistan, the second at Emba in Kazakhstan, the third at Sterlitamak, a hundred miles west of Magnitogorsk, the fourth at Ghusovaya near Perm in the northern Urals, and the last on the small river Usa (a tributary of the Pechora) in an uninhabited Arctic pine forest. This chain of oil supplies, when fully developed, will be of immense value to the industries of the Urals and for the mechanized farming of Eastern Russia. Other minor oilfields are being developed in Uzbekistan and Tadzhikistan as well as at various places in Western Russia. In the Far East there is reported to be oil in the volcanic peninsula of Kamchatka, while the island of Sakhalin, hitherto divided as to ownership between Russia and Japan, has oilfields that have been worked for many years, but with only a small output. The Soviets have constructed a pipe line to the mainland, and have set up refining centres there so that such oil as there is can be put to speedy local use instead of being carried away in its crude state to remote refineries. Before the war a new refinery was under construction at Komsomolsk near the mouth of the river Amur. This new town has sprung up in a few years, and is now about the size of one of the smaller industrial towns of Great Britain. It is intended to be the Magnitogorsk of Russia's Far

East, supplying all the Pacific regions with their machinery requirements. It appears, however, that the local iron and coal, of which there were thought to be adequate supplies, are both inferior in quality and that the town is at present dependent on supplies from afar.

If iron and oil are the industrial defences of a nation, gold is often the only means of paying for them. The Soviets have therefore increased the exploitation of the gold supplies of Siberia to such an extent that the U.S.S.R. is sometimes reckoned to hold the third place in output, after South Africa and Canada, and by some is considered to come next after South Africa. The Soviet Government has guarded the secret of its total gold output. It is quite clear, in any case, that since Russia does not need gold as the basis of her own managed currency, she has adequate supplies to pay for foreign goods in so far as these outweigh her exports.

NEW DEVELOPMENTS

Before concluding this brief examination of Russia's new and more important industrial defences, we must at least draw attention to other new industrial developments which may soon contribute more substantially to her armoury, or which even now are bringing to the people of the U.S.S.R. material changes undreamed of a generation ago. There are, for instance, a host of industrial enterprises in Soviet Asia apart from the oil and coal fields already mentioned. The minerals below the deserts, plains and mountain sides of these eastern republics seem endless—gold, silver, lead, copper, zinc, diamonds and radium are found in the official lists, and mines for all of them are in action or projected. Almost as long a list would apply to Siberia, where scattered settlements among the pine forests are the beginnings of new industrial towns. And yet again there are the desolate polar regions where Soviet geologists, camping on the ice and fed with supplies brought by aeroplanes, have been plotting out the hidden frozen minerals. These, too, may be an invitation to the next generation of Soviet citizens.

The tremendous increase in cotton growing and in textile manufacture must also not be forgotten; it is, in fact, one of the outstanding successes of the Soviets that they have extended the national cotton supplies to equal the country's need, whereas formerly half Russia's cotton was imported. The industry flourishes in Central Asia, particularly in Uzbekistan, where irrigation has turned the desert into cotton fields, and where the ancient city of Tashkent has a suburb of cotton mills. Finally, there is the national scheme of electrification. This was Lenin's dream as far back as 1918. "Lenin," said H. G. Wells after a visit to the Kremlin in 1920, "is throwing all his weight into a scheme for the development of great power stations in Russia, to serve whole provinces with light, water transport and mill-power." Wells confessed that he found the project a "strain upon the constructive imagination. I cannot see anything of the sort happening," he said, "in this dark crystal of Russia." The electrification plan, however, is already virtually accomplished. Power stations are found in every region, and are fed by local supplies—coal dust, peat or water power. Every one now knows how the rapids of the river Dnieper were turned to good account by a mammoth dam; similar projects are intended for the Volga.

Thus it comes about that there is a supply of electric power for all the new industrial areas, and in remote Soviet villages, whether in the Siberian forests, or on the banks of the great rivers, or in the expanses of steppe land, the traveller is likely to find the peasants supplied with electric light. This brings us back to the peasantry, who still make up 80 per cent of the population of the U.S.S.R., and to their very important share in the reorganization of Russia under the Plans.

THE COLLECTIVIZATION OF AGRICULTURE

In 1928, when the first Five-Year Plan was put into action, there were something like twenty-four million peasant holdings in Russia, many of them very small and scattered in strips, often at some distance from the owner's home. They were worked on the simplest methods, and many of them lacked even a horse to draw the plough. They were, although legally the property of the State, virtually the possession of the peasant families, and each strip was marked off from its neighbours by a ridge and unsown furrow. To acquire the land for themselves had been for the peasants the one and only political idea of the revolution, and even before the Bolsheviks had come to power they were seizing the property of the landlords and dividing it among themselves, at the same time revengefully burning the houses of the former landed gentry and often valuable farm equipment at the same time.

But the first ten years of Communism brought the peasants anything but prosperity. War, famine and the Government's requisitions of grain had left a trail of misery. Only during the N.E.P. period, when there were manufactured goods to be bought with their surplus stocks, did they begin to recover, and even so, they had little but a bare independence. It was a purpose of the first Five-Year Plan to take this independence away. In a socialist State the private ownership of farms was not to be countenanced, and it was only because it was the most difficult of all the acts of revolution that the socialization of farming had been postponed. The determination to industrialize Russia made the reorganization of agriculture an immediate necessity. The industrial populations of the new towns must be fed and the uneconomic system of millions of small farms, individually owned, was not the cheapest or most rational way of supplying their food. Everything pointed to the mechanization of agriculture, to tractor-drawn ploughs, mechanized harvesters and threshing machines. Such agricultural machinery would be made in the new factories, but it could only be used on large scale farms. There were two ways in which the farms could be enlarged and socialized. Peasant holdings could be abolished and supplanted by large State farms, organized in the same way as State industries; or the peasants could be induced to co-operate in large collective farms. Both methods had been tried on a small scale, but it was the collective farm or *kolkhoz* which was finally selected by the Communist Party and the Government.

On paper the Plan was simple. A minimum of fifteen neighbouring farms would voluntarily agree to merge their holdings. This was merely a beginning, and other farms in the district would ask to come into the collective as time went on and as the advantages of the new Plan became apparent. Each peasant in joining the collective would not only pool his land but also his stock, seeds and agricultural implements. All that he brought in would be assessed in value and would bring him a proportional share of the proceeds of the collective—a principle which did not, however, materialize. The large joint farm would then become the collective property of all the peasant members who would organize it themselves. They would elect a committee of management, with chairman and secretary, and also a smaller committee of inspectors. The different kinds of work to be done, the milking, carting, ploughing, and so on, would be undertaken by members of the collective working in brigades under elected leaders and in accordance with the directions of the committee of management. The Government would advance credits for the erection of new farm buildings and for other initial requirements, while from the Motor Tractor Stations, about to be established by the Government all over the country, tractors and harvester combines would be lent out as needed. For this last service the collective would pay the Motor Tractor Station a fixed amount of produce, and once the new farm was established it would have to sell to the Government, at low fixed prices, a certain proportion of its grain and crops—and of its livestock if it had any. The remaining produce would be divided among the members of the *kolkhoz* according to the number of "labour days" worked and the nature of the work performed. Or, alternatively, some of it might be sold in the unrestricted peasant market and the proceeds divided on the same basis.

Much would be done for the ease and recreation of the collective members. A canteen and clubrooms would be provided for the men and women workers and a crêche and nursery to accommodate their small children while they worked. Moreover, each peasant family would retain its own cottage and a garden plot. Later on, after the development of a slower and more sympathetic policy, instituted by Stalin (see below) the size of this individual homestead was fixed from about one-quarter of an acre to three acres, according to the nature of the soil, and the number of personal livestock was settled at from one to three cows, and any number of pigs, chickens and bees.

This new programme, with its promises of prosperity, the agents of the Government and the appointed Party men took from the Capital to the scattered peasantry, and before long

F

the *kolkhoz* was the prevailing topic of conversation in every village. An important part of the propaganda now let loose on the peasants included an attack on those among them who were better off and who were now referred to as *kulaks*. The word, which carries the meaning of a fist, had in pre-Revolution days been applied to a small class of prosperous peasants who had hired labour in the manner of small landlords. It was from an outsider's point of view an unfair perversion to include under one name all those peasants who had most successfully weathered the recent years of bewilderment and difficulty. Some of them no doubt gained advantage by peasant cunning carried to doubtful lengths, but others had taken advantage of the relative freedom of the N.E.P. period to provide security for themselves and their children. Although they were the least likely of all the peasants to welcome the new collectives, they were not even given the opportunity to join them. To the rest of the peasants they were held up as parasites, crafty self-seekers, and dangers to the State. They were caricatured on posters either as bloated gluttons or as deceitful and hypercritical counter-revolutionaries. It was, indeed, part of the Soviet Government's policy to remove them altogether. Their grounds for so doing were that their existence would provoke dissatisfaction in the new collectives, for as long as an example of prosperous individual peasant-ownership could be seen, other peasants might wish to try to emulate them. Thus, the whole drive towards co-operative a against individual farming would be weakened from the start The *kulaks*, therefore (who numbered, according to Soviet figures, one million families), were banished into Eastern Russia where they were ultimately reinstated as citizens and found employment in State industries. A great number of them are said to have perished.

To the abuse of the *kulaks* and the fair promises of the *kolkhoz* the ordinary peasants listened with stolid scepticism. In groups in the village streets, or gathered round the stove in a cottage, or assembled in the open air to listen to a speech delivered by a man from Moscow, they showed little enthusiasm. For the most part only the younger people were willing to be enrolled as *kolkhoz* members, and although the tireless explanations of the Government missionaries gradually wore down the instinctive objections of the poorest and less able peasants, it did not seem likely that collective farms manned by inexperience and incompetence were likely to succeed. Yet, to cut short the long story of struggle between Government and peasantry, the collective did in the end succeed, and not only became the prevailing system of agriculture throughout the U.S.S.R., but after a preliminary period when production declined, brought a steady increase first in crops and afterwards in livestock also.

Taxation and threats played their part in driving the peasants to form up in the collectives. Rather than be excommunicated from the new order in Russia their natural conservatism gave way. At first the change-over to socialist farming was produced too rapidly by the enthusiasts and the sullen mood of the peasants, especially in those districts where the promised Motor Tractor Stations had not yet appeared, caused misgivings in the capital. Protests poured in to the Government, and Stalin in a famous letter to the press entitled "Dizzy with Success," rebuked the promoters of the new farms for over-enthusiasm, and called for a steadier advance. Farms that had been forcibly collectivized were dissolved at the Government's orders. A new emphasis on the private homesteads of the collective members helped to bring about a different attitude among the peasants, but when later on it was found that in many cases the peasants were spending more time on these than on the joint farm, new decrees had to be issued stipulating a minimum number of "labour days" to be given to the collective, and making the proportion of produce to be sold at low rates to the Government more comprehensive. One of the later decrees insisted on a contribution of livestock from every farm. This cancelled a former arrangement by which a collective need only give livestock if it was a stock farm and it enforced a healthy development of mixed farming.

The position to-day is some sort of balance between individual initiative and enforced public service. The need to pay Government taxes, supply the full list of Government requirements in farm produce, and pay, also in produce, for the services of the Motor Tractor Stations, together with the stipulated number of "labour days" to be given to the collective in a year, is the sum total of enforced service. On the other hand, the opportunities of the private homestead and the right of the peasant to sell his private produce in the free market, not at Government-fixed prices but for what it will fetch, satisfies to some extent the age-long instincts of personal enterprise in the peasant. In this connection it is interesting to note that the divergence between the prices paid by the Government for its requisitions and those fetched in the free markets is enormous, the market prices being sometimes one hundred times the Government prices. The Government, of course, uses the supplies that it acquires thus cheaply to furnish the town shops with cheap food for the industrial workers.

RESULTS OF THE PLANS

Before concluding this section it is necessary to look at the results of the period of planning. Here we shall only be concerned with the national estimates of increasing output. The effects of the Plans on the lives of the people properly belong to the next chapter.

The diagrams given on pages 84—85 speak for themselves, and in almost any item selected the progress appears astonishing. It is generally considered that by the time the first Five-Year Plan was put into action Russia had recovered from the devastations of war, civil war, and revolution, and that her production level stood approximately where it had been in 1913. Any comparisons between 1913 and the immediate pre-war period, therefore, may be taken as the rate of increase under the Plans.

The diagrams show that the annual output of coal had increased by more than five times, of steel by more than four times, of machine tools by more than forty times, and of chemical products by more than twelve times. This progress is the more interesting when it is remembered that the years 1929 to 1937 (that is, the period of the first two Plans) were the years of the worst economic crisis that the world has known, and that production in other countries declined in most commodities. It is not surprising therefore that we find the U.S.S.R. outstripping other countries and taking a much higher place than formerly in the relative position of the different nations in world production of raw materials and manufactured goods. In coal production the U.S.S.R. rises from the sixth place in 1913 to fourth place in 1937, in pig iron from the fifth place to the second place, in gold from a negligible place to the second or third place (exact figures are not available); in oil she maintains the second place, in spite of a general increase in other countries; in electrical power she rises from the fifteenth place to the second place; in agricultural engineering, aluminium and superphosphates

from no place at all to second place; and in copper from
seventh place to first place. In total industrial production
there is a rise from the fifth to the third place. Again, if the
rate of increase in general production in the U.S.S.R. be
compared (see page 84) with the rate of increase in Germany
which, after Russia, made more advance than any other
country, it will be found that whereas German total production had risen by about one-quarter between 1929 and 1938,
Russian production had increased five-fold.

From the point of view of the Soviet Government the increased output, astonishing as it is, was not altogether satisfactory, for the output per head of Soviet workers was less
than the output per head elsewhere. There were very good
reasons for this. The vast majority of the industrial workers
in present-day Russia yesterday were peasants, herdsmen or
nomads, and a great many of them were illiterate. Again, the
very immensity of the national Plans brought a certain amount
of waste. Many mistakes were made in the early stages. Engineering plants were erected to be fed by local raw materials
that afterwards were found to be inadequate, and sometimes
a works dependent on both machine tools and raw materials
would get the one without the other. Further, the very nature
of planning involves a mass of calculations not only at the
centre but at every point in the industrial field, and this means
the employment of a far larger number of administrative and
clerical workers than capitalist industry finds necessary. And
finally the size of the country had put a strain on transport, so
that in spite of new roads, many new canals connecting up
seas and rivers and such railway developments as the double
tracking of the Trans-Siberian railway through its entire
length, the increase in the burden of goods to be carried was
at first greater than the increase in the means of carrying

them. This, however, was felt much more in the earlier than in the later days of planning, and the successful equipment of vast Soviet armies in the war against Germany showed that the initial difficulties had been triumphantly overcome.

A great effort was made in the course of the third Five-Year Plan to speed up the average production per worker by such means as the development of the piece system, and by awarding honours to "Stakhanovites" or record-breaking heroes. The triumphs of industry are a constant feature of the Soviet press where the heroes of industry are honoured no less than the heroes of war.

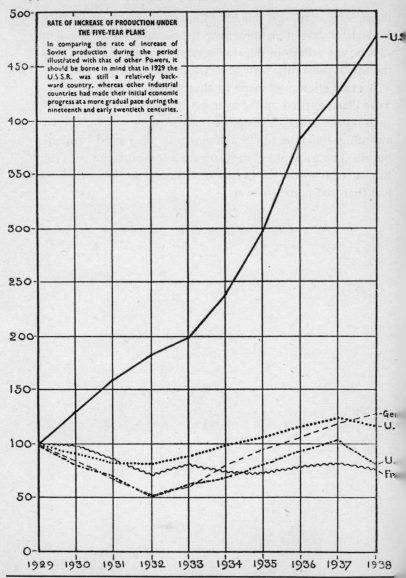

84

RATE OF INCREASE OF PRODUCTION UNDER
THE FIVE-YEAR PLANS

In comparing the rate of increase of
Soviet production during the period
illustrated with that of other Powers, it
should be borne in mind that in 1929 the
U.S.S.R. was still a relatively backward country, whereas other industrial
countries had made their initial economic
progress at a more gradual pace during the
nineteenth and early twentieth centuries.

RATE OF INCREASE OF PRODUCTION UNDER THE FIVE-YEAR PL

INCREASES IN SOVIET PRODUCTION

A Selected List of Commodities Based on Approximate Figures

	1913	1940
Oil [million tons]	9	34
Coal [million tons]	29	164
Steel [million tons]	4	18
Machine Tools [thousands]	1	48
Chemicals [million roubles]	450	5944
Grain [million tons]	80	119
Sugar Beet [million tons]	10	21
Raw Cotton [million tons]	0·7	2
Electricity [million Kilowatts]	2	36

Fig. for 1937

INCREASE IN LITERACY

1913	1940
28%	81%

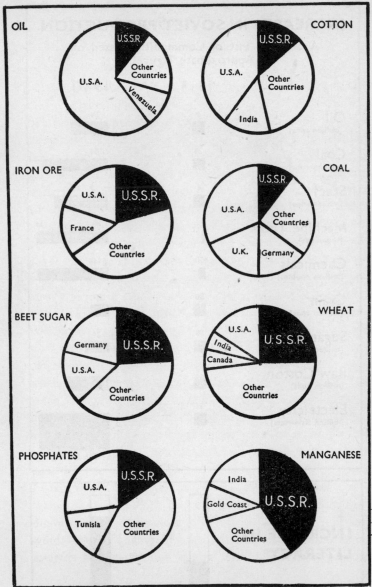

SOVIET SHARE OF WORLD PRODUCTION (1938)

V

LIVING CONDITIONS IN THE U.S.S.R.

"THEY promise us everything for to-morrow," complained an old Russian peasant to an American visiting his village at the beginning of the first Five-Year Plan. It was the natural comment of an old man, born and bred in a hand-to-mouth existence, on a revolutionary government that was prepared to uproot him and reorganize him in the interests of the future. But what to him was a reproach was to others of his compatriots a spur and a hope. Since the Bolsheviks achieved their victory, and more particularly since the beginning of the Plans, Russia has been essentially a land of to-morrow. The Soviet leaders set themselves to accomplish in twenty years a process of industrialization that would exceed what other countries had achieved in a century and a half. Convinced that before this period had run out the enemy would cross their frontiers, they ordered a speeding-up which necessitated meagre living and left a track of what seemed to the casual visitor to be neglected or unfinished workmanship. "What is a drip of snow, after all?" asked an enthusiastic Soviet citizen when a foreign traveller complained of a faulty ventilator in the railway carriage. "We have far more important things to attend to." And to another visitor who asked about pot-holes in the pavements of Moscow another Soviet citizen gave a similar answer: "We concentrate on the things that *matter*. What have pot-holes to do with progress?" Such incidents belong to the years before the war when many obvious things were neglected while other things, sometimes less obvious, were changing. It was no uncommon experience to meet this indifference to small discomforts, especially among the younger Russians. Russia was in fact experiencing war conditions without being at war, and many found happiness in losing themselves in the great collective venture which the Plans represented.

THE INDUSTRIAL WORKER

Nevertheless, the mass of the people in the U.S.S.R. as in other countries are probably more disposed to look for happiness in immediate actualities than in distant prospects. How far have everyday conditions of living been improved for these ordinary people by the Soviet system, and how do they compare with living conditions elsewhere? Let us consider, for instance, a worker in one of the new Soviet factories, and inquire what the Soviet State has so far done for him. The casual visitor to Russia may be inclined to think it has not done much. He does not appear very different from millions of other industrial workers in other countries. He is one of a drab crowd flocking through the factory gates at the beginning of the day and coming out in the same hurried manner at the end. Patiently as those others in other countries he queues up for tram or train and later makes his way to a block of workers' flats which, if it is one of the latest Soviet designs, will stand comparison with the best in Western Europe. But his own home in this warren of dwellings will lack the minor luxuries of the British artisan home—the private radio, the open hearth, the variety of cheap articles from Woolworths; and the living space available for himself and his family will be small. Housing construction in Russia has lagged behind the needs of the people and it is still not uncommon for two or more families to share one flat. It is likely, also, that both the man's home and the town in which he lives and works will

appear hastily constructed or even unfinished. Some of the
roads may be little more than muddy tracks; where there is a
lift it may be out of order; doors and windows may not fit, and
the painting of woodwork may be unfinished. These, at all
events, were the impressions of the foreign visitor before the
war; but these defects were rapidly disappearing.

Housing, however, was not neglected; it had to take its
place in the national scheme, and behind conditions which
are obviously less comfortable than in England or America,
there are benefits which the workers of pre-revolutionary
Russia could never hope to enjoy. The chief of these is security of employment. The Five-Year Plans swept away the fear
of being out of work—the worst of all the strains of poverty—
and the Soviet Government declares that its system of a
planned economy has banished it for ever. For this reason
the unemployment insurance scheme which was introduced
in the earlier days of the regime has been abolished, and if
some reorganization or dislocation brings a man's job in a
particular factory to an end it is the responsibility of his
trade union to find him another.

Although unemployment insurance has been abolished as
unnecessary, other forms of social insurance have been developed. In the case of sickness or accident the worker will
receive immediate benefit that will vary in amount according
to the nature of his work. Moreover, sickness in his family
will be covered by the same scheme as that which provides
against his own personal misfortunes. Allowances are graded
in accordance with the worker's term of service in his place
of work. For instance, after two years' service the benefit
amounts to 60 per cent of his wages, but after six years he
will receive the amount of his full wages. The funds from
which the payments are made are supplied entirely by the

industrial enterprise in which the worker is employed, and the insurance fund is based on a percentage of the wages paid out; the worker, therefore, makes no direct contribution. This arrangement contrasts with the usual one in other countries, whereby the industrial enterprise, the worker and the State are joint contributors.

These insurance funds, covering not only illness and accidents, but funeral benefits, maternity benefits, old age and widows' pensions, and convalescent holidays, are entirely in the hands of the trade unions, and it is by virtue of his trade union membership that the worker acquires his right to help from them. His trade union will also, as in other countries, watch over his wages and negotiate for advances, but such negotiations will not be in the nature of a test of strength between opposing parties, and strikes are illegal. They will be largely concerned with the readjustment of piece rates, for the piece rate system prevails throughout Russian industry.

Before the war the Russian worker had, according to law, a shorter working day and a longer holiday than was common elsewhere. The usual arrangement (although exceptions were frequently permitted) was a seven-hour day, a "rest day" after every six days, and a minimum of two weeks' holiday in the year. These provisions, however, were swept aside under the necessity of increased output for war purposes. For the worker's leisure time the Soviet Government has made special provision. Every trade union provides its clubrooms and every sizeable town has its parks, its athletic clubs, libraries, educational classes, cinema, theatre, and very often its stadium. Moreover, all the trade unions have large holiday homes among the Caucasian mountains or by the shores of the Black Sea, and here the worker can spend the annual holiday, if he is lucky enough to be sent free of charge as a reward for distinction in his work or if he can afford the cost and secure the accommodation. In actual fact, since there are not yet enough holiday homes to meet the needs of the vast industrial population, only a small proportion of the workers have, up to the present, been able to enjoy the pleasures of these resorts.

It would be a mistake to think of the average Russian worker as necessarily the sole or even the chief breadwinner in the family. More often than not his wife will be a factory worker also, and since the rates of pay for men and women are the same, it is always possible that she may bring home a larger wage than her husband. Of all the social changes brought about under Soviet rule, none are perhaps so marked as those which affect women. In every respect men and women are equal under Soviet law and in order that a woman's function of child-bearing shall not be a handicap in her industrial life, nor suffer under it, certain regulations have to be observed by all Soviet enterprises employing women. A pregnant woman must be given a holiday of at least one month before childbirth, followed by another period of one month afterwards, and during this time her wages must be paid. On resuming work, the mother may leave her baby in the crêche attached to the factory and the management must release her to suckle the child at the appropriate intervals. For older children there will almost certainly be a nursery, so that there is nothing to prevent the wife and mother from continuing with her industrial life for so long as she chooses to do so. Like her husband, she will belong to a trade union, and as a member of this she will have the same opportunity as the male workers to choose the factory committee or be elected to it herself. As her children reach the age of eight they will leave the factory nursery for the local school and there they will normally remain until the age of fifteen.

The children's mid-day meal may be provided at school just as it was formerly provided in the factory nursery, and if on holidays the family chooses to leave the crowded home for a day in the local park of Rest and Culture, among the various entertainments provided there will be special recreational opportunities for children, including possibly a children's theatre or a children's cinema. There may also be a crèche and nursery where the smallest children may be left. The married woman is thus not only given the opportunity of earning an independent income if she wishes, but also of taking the rest which she may need.

EDUCATION

The care and education of children have been one of the main pre-occupations of the Soviet leaders. The rates of maternity and infantile mortality have been greatly reduced by the provisions now made for the pregnant mother and her child. The new industrial towns have their lying-in hospitals, and it is interesting to note that the maternity benefit includes the provision of a layette for the baby. Crèches and nurseries, although not yet as universal as the paper plans envisage, are well equipped and well supervised wherever they occur. The entertainments provided in public parks for older children are often both ingenious and instructive—as for instance the mock Arctic tour which was laid out in the Moscow Park of Rest and Culture. Here some of the Soviet polar explorers met the children on their journey and explained to them the purpose of the original expedition.

Compulsory education had only been accepted as a national policy in Russia a little time before the first world war—fifty years later than in Great Britain. The Soviet Government was therefore faced with the need to build an educational system almost from the beginning and confronted with an adult population that was largely illiterate. Its efforts to deal with this situation must be reckoned among its major achievements. Nowadays there are schools all over the U.S.S.R., and it may be assumed that virtually all Soviet children are receiving free elementary education from the ages of eight to fifteen. The schools were co-educational until 1943, when a decree changed this; boys and girls are now taught separately. In secondary schools and all higher educational institutions fees are now charged except in special cases. The course followed is not dissimilar from that in other countries, but there are certain special features. No religious instruction is given, a measure of Communist doctrine is imparted, and there is a bias in favour of scientific subjects. A great number of technical schools have been established to meet the needs of the new industries and under a recent decree boys are liable to be called up at fourteen or sixteen for a technical training. There are various indications that school life under the Soviets is popular. This is admitted by those who are disposed to criticize the Soviet system and Soviet teaching; one of them, for instance, has reported on the way in which children attending the new schools in Soviet Asia tried to elude parents who seek to keep them at home.

Throughout the U.S.S.R. there are voluntary schools for adults. In the past many of these have been chiefly concerned with teaching men and women to read and write, and there has been widespread enthusiasm on the part of both teachers and taught to combat illiteracy. There are other opportunities for those who have passed beyond the stage of literacy, in particular, classes in technical subjects. There is also, of course, every encouragement for the Soviet citizen to learn

G

about the significance of the Revolution and to be interested
in the progress of the Soviet State. Books on Marxist doctrine
are to be found in every clubroom and library and every
factory has its own newspaper wherein is discussed the factory's own part in planned production. In large enterprises
this will be printed, in small factories it will be a large notice-
board referred to as the "wall newspaper."

There has been an enthusiastic response to the efforts of the
Soviet Government to awaken a desire for further education
among the adult population, but even those who are not interested cannot altogether escape some kind of instruction.
There are, for instance, the informative posters encouraging a
higher standard of household hygiene, including pictorial
warnings against fly-borne disease; in public parks one may
meet gigantic reeling figures designed to show the results of
over-drinking, and across the streets of Soviet cities hang
slogan banners urging the advantages of national savings and
subscriptions to Government loans.

THE PEASANTS

So far we have concentrated on life in the industrial towns;
but the greater part of the population of the U.S.S.R. live in
villages. What benefits has the revolutionary regime brought
to these peasants, and what does the collective farm system
mean for those who have been swept into it?

In the first place, it has brought to them, as planning has
brought to the industrial worker, a new security. As an individual farmer with a very small holding the peasant was formerly
at the mercy of sudden disaster. A bad harvest or the loss of
his only horse or cow might bring him to ruin. Now the greater yield from large-scale mechanized farms assures him a live-
lihood which he can supplement from his private farmstead.

Bad weather conditions and the other hazards to which farming the world over is subject still contribute an element of uncertainty to his life. However poor the harvest yield and whatever misfortunes may befall the collective livestock, the Government requisitions must be produced and the local Motor Traction Station must be paid for its services. In bad years there may be little left over to share among the collective members for private use or for sale. Nevertheless, the members will have been supplied with their day-to-day requirements of food and the homestead remains each family's private preserve. Again, the collective provides for its members in case of sickness and infirmity in the same way that the Trade Union meets these eventualities in the factory. The collective will also normally have its crêche and nursery to enable the married women to work in the farm if they so wish.

All this means a very substantial improvement in the material conditions of the Russian peasant to-day as compared with those of the peasant under the Tsars, and there is little doubt that the younger generation finds the *kolkhoz* much more to its liking than the individual peasant system that prevailed during the first ten years of the Revolution. The older peasants may still regret the loss of their independence, insecure though it was, and these regrets will necessarily be embittered when the leaders of the farming brigades and the committee members of the farm are young and intolerant, or again when the farm suffers from disharmony and poor organization. One collective farm is not the same as another, and through the length and breadth of Russia the standards vary considerably. There is no doubt that for a great many peasants the private homestead is apt to be regarded as more important than the *kolkhoz*. A few years before the war, when the Government instituted a nation-wide inspection into the collective system, it was found that in some instances the peasants were putting in very little time on the collective farm and devoting almost all their energies to their private holdings. Now a minimum number of "labour days" must be put in on the collective farms, but the number—which varies according to locality—is not onerous and still leaves ample time for the peasant to attend to his own plot, his pigs and chickens and his cow. Since he also lives in his own cottage in the village he still preserves some of the independence of the individual peasant, and despite collective meals taken on labour days with a group of his fellow workers and the attractions of the clubroom and of entertainments provided for the collective members, the married peasants still maintain a private family life within the large group.

FAMILY LIFE AND RELIGION

Family life in Russia to-day is certainly not impaired by the social changes introduced under the Soviet system. The family is always a strong social unit in a peasant country, and it is not the policy of the Soviet Government to try to weaken it. The irresponsibility with which partnerships were undertaken in the early years of the Revolution is now condemned, stability in the marriage relationship is encouraged, and although divorce is a simpler process than in some other countries, it is not regarded as something to be entered upon lightly, a steeply increasing fee being charged after the first occasion. Again, Soviet law enforces the responsibility of the father towards children born from a previous marriage or outside matrimony, requiring him to contribute to their support.

Marriage may still be celebrated in a church, but it is only the civil marriage registered before State authorities that is recognized. This is in accordance with the Soviet attitude towards religion. This attitude has changed considerably in the course of a quarter of a century. It was at first definitely hostile, then in 1936 the new Constitution permitted both "freedom of religious worship and freedom of anti-religious propaganda"; at the same time it restored the voting rights of priests who had hitherto been disenfranchised. Later anti-religious propaganda came to an end. Finally, in September 1943, the leaders of the Orthodox Church in the Soviet Union were allowed to reorganize their church on its former basis. The church, however, remains a disestablished church; in other words it is quite separate from the State. It is not yet clear what is to be the status of the Roman Catholics and the various nonconformist sects who had their place in the old regime but whose leaders were sent to Siberia or obliged to flee the country.

An uncompromising distrust of religion on the part of Russian Communists was held by them to be necessary to the building of the Soviet State. It was considered that within the Party itself religious belief would have interfered with that single-minded obedience to the Communist faith which Party discipline required, while for the mass of the people it was the Communist view that religion offered a narcotic which would detract from the appeal of the classless society. The Communists constantly reminded the people that the Russian Orthodox Church had been customarily against social reform, and that the blessing of the crops by village priests was formerly considered more important than crop rotation and fertilizers. For these charges there was some basis. It would, indeed, be hardly unfair to say that the same inertia which prevented the former rulers of Russia from fulfilling their responsibilities towards the Russian people was found in the Russian Church, although the church went some way towards meeting particular needs of the Russian temperament. On holy days it offered a rich spectacle; it provided the means of solemnizing birth, marriage and death, and at the appropriate seasons it gave its blessings to work in the fields. But it did not concern itself overmuch with the personal conduct, the deeper aspirations, or the material conditions of its adherents. As an integral part of the Tsarist system it collapsed with it, and what remained was not a church but scattered churches where those who had not been convinced by Communist argument continued to worship. Similarly, in Asiatic Russia hundreds of mosques still met the needs of the Moslems. For the most part, however, it was the older Soviet citizens who kept up their religious observances, while among the younger generation there was found that self-dedication to the Soviet State which one of the most competent observers of the revolutionary regime has described as the "fervour of the faithful."

In spite, then, of the legal right to religious worship, it remains true that the full weight of official disapproval is thrown against it. Religion was regarded as an enemy of the regime, and was thrust aside along with all other obstacles—the friends of the old regime who hoped for its restoration, the N.E.P. men who outstayed their usefulness, the kulaks, the Trotskyites, and Communists who lost their faith.

SOVIET DEMOCRACY

This casting aside of everything that does not fit into the system prescribed by the Soviets has provoked a great deal of criticism in the western democracies, and although loyalty to a great ally silenced obstinate questionings during the war years, they are likely to be voiced again. In Britain and the United States the magnificent achievement of the Soviet

Union in building up in so short a time an industrial and military power capable of inflicting defeat on the German armies is now fully recognized and applauded. But since in these countries and elsewhere democracy has been almost synonymous with political liberty—with its ancillary rights of free speech and free association—the Soviet Union with its single Party, its controlled press and its remorseless penalties for criticism of the Party line, does not seem to fit into the picture of a democratic state. From the Soviet Union's point of view, however, democracy is not a matter of political liberty but of economic opportunity—and to this there has lately been added the concept of anti-Fascism. In the Russia of to-day all industry is organized by State enterprise and, except for those who are privileged to have domestic servants or other similar forms of personal and state-regulated assistance, there are no private employers. It naturally follows that there are no investments outside Soviet Government bonds and the Soviet National Savings schemes. Thus, despite the very great differences in income due to the Soviet policy of rewarding skill and achievement at every level, there is economic equality in the sense that economic advantages are open to all and that all are working as servants of the State.

A point that is sometimes overlooked is that there seems to be no desire among the people of the Soviet Union for that free speech for which our ancestors fought and which has long been dearly prized by British people. This is not surprising when it is remembered that free speech is not something taken from the Russians by their present rulers, but something which the Russians have never had. Nor is there any evidence, despite the natural bent of the Russian for metaphysical enquiry and his lively curiosity in other countries, that he resents a political outlook superimposed from above. We have, in fact, been thrown by the war into close association with a Power and a people whose political values are not necessarily better or worse, but essentially different from our own.

VI

SOVIET FOREIGN RELATIONS

1. BETWEEN THE WARS IN EUROPE

IT IS clearly impossible in one short chapter to deal circumstantially with the relations between the Soviet Union and other countries during the twenty-nine years which have passed since the Soviet Revolution. On the other hand, any attempt to clarify the picture of the U.S.S.R. leaves much still obscure if it confines itself to internal policies, their execution and subsequent results for the Russian people. This obscurity is increased by the dust-storms that constantly arose when the Soviet's revolutionary regime impinged, or threatened to impinge, on the outer world. It is neither possible nor profitable to try to tidy up all the débris left behind by these impacts, but considering these contentious years in retrospect, it may prove possible to show the changing purposes of Soviet foreign policy in Europe between the two wars. For reasons of space the account is confined to one continent. As to Soviet foreign policy during the second World War, a bare record of events, in so far as they can be ascertained, will be stated.

No country's foreign policy is entirely unrelated to its internal policy, but in the case of the Soviet Union the two policies have been so integrated as to be two facets of the same purpose. This fact helps to explain both the attitude and actions of the Soviet Government during the period under review, and is the clue to the former mutual distrust and suspicion between the Soviet Union and those who are now her allies. It also, incidentally, explains why it has already been necessary to include some reference to Soviet foreign policy in previous chapters on internal development.

During the first eleven years of the Soviet regime Soviet foreign policy was determined, at first actually and afterwards still nominally, by the Bolshevik doctrine of world revolution; during the second eleven years the pursuit of peaceful relations, already begun as a necessity, became a definite enduring policy as a result of Stalin's conception of "socialism in one State" and the inauguration of the Five-Year Plans. In 1939 there came the sudden and short-lived pact with Germany, abruptly ended when the Germans brought Russia into the war by the invasion of her territory in June 1941. The subject of this chapter, therefore, falls naturally into four parts, each dealing with a new development in Russia's foreign relations.

1917—1928

The first act of the Bolshevik Government towards a foreign Power was to negotiate with Germany for the termination of hostilities. This, as we have seen, was in fulfilment of the Bolshevik promise of peace, but it was also doubtless necessary for the continued existence of the regime, which could hardly hope to establish itself at home and continue a war abroad at the same time. Lenin hoped to secure a generous peace, but the German leaders took advantage of the situation to secure for themselves, directly or indirectly, the rich lands of Western Russia. Had not the treaty of Brest Litovsk been invalidated by the German collapse and annulled by the Peace Conference in Paris, Russia would have ceded the Baltic States and Russian Poland to Germany and Austria-Hungary, certain Caucasian territories to Turkey, while recognizing the independence (under German guarantee) of Finland, Ukraine and Georgia.

From the point of view of Lenin and his associates—some of whom, indeed, were at first unwilling to sign away so much of Russian territory—the price of peace was relatively unimportant, since they expected to see all frontiers become insignificant before a universal rising of the proletariat. The Allies took a different view. Armed forces were sent to Russia, at first to attack the Germans, but afterwards to support the counter-revolutionaries—the "Whites"—and when the Peace Conference met in Paris the Russians were not asked to send representatives, although at one point Mr Lloyd George seems to have been willing to make contact between the Conference and the Bolshevik Government. In the final event the territories which Russia had agreed at Brest Litovsk to cede to the Central Powers—with the exception of the Ukraine, Georgia and the Caucasian territories—became independent States, and were regarded by some as buffers between the new revolutionary Russia and western Europe. M. Clemenceau described them as a "Cordon Sanitaire." This point of view was the argument used by Poland in seeking the British Government's acceptance of the new Russo-Polish frontier—a good deal further east than the proposed "Curzon Line"—which Poland claimed from Russia after the struggle which ended in the Peace of Riga (March 1921). Allied intervention on behalf of the counter-revolutionaries continued until 1921 when it was abandoned. It had not met with much success and it was very unpopular with the working people of Britain. Its justification from the Allied point of view depended on various facts—the Bolshevik conviction that world revolution was both imminent and to be encouraged ("Workers of the world, Unite!"); the Bolshevik cancellation of foreign debts; the fear of a Russo-German alliance; and the violence of the political, economic and social changes inside Russia. In Allied eyes all these constituted a serious threat to world stability after the defeat of Germany.

The end of intervention in Russia did not result in the establishment of normal relations between the Soviet Government and other Powers. Even though Lenin's conviction of the imminence of world revolution might have been considered disproved after the collapse of the revolutionary movements in Germany and Bulgaria in 1923, and finally interred after Chiang-Kai-Shek's break with the Chinese Communists in 1927, and although the Russian leaders showed themselves now anxious to establish commercial and diplomatic relations, distrust and aloofness was the prevailing attitude of other Governments. In this they were encouraged by the suspicions which arose from the activities of the Comintern. This, the "Third International," was created on the initiative of the Bolshevik or Communist Party of Russia, and became a federation of Communist parties all over the world. The headquarters were in Moscow, and since all national Communist parties accepted and advocated the policies of the Russian Communists, it was generally assumed, rightly or wrongly, that Communists everywhere were under the direction of the Soviet Government. It thus came about that the Soviet Union seemed to have two contradictory policies. As has been said, the Soviet leaders were now anxious to conclude agreements with other nations. This, in fact, was their main concern, and necessary for the succour of their people who had endured war, civil war and famine. But at the same time national Communist parties stood for world revolution.

This apparent ambiguity in Russia's foreign relations fostered the hostility and mistrust which had already been provoked by the revolution, and throughout the 1920's the process of re-establishing foreign relations proceeded slowly and with set-backs. In the case of Great Britain a trade agreement was negotiated in 1921, but full relations and recognition were not established until the Labour Government came to power early in 1924. In October of the same year the Labour Government was forced to resign, and during the subsequent election campaign great publicity was given to a letter which it was said came from the Comintern headquarters in Moscow under the signature of Zinoviev, secretary to the Comintern. There was considerable doubt as to the authenticity of the letter, and some plainly declared it to be a forgery. The incident, however, strengthened the case of those who had protested against the British Government's recognition of the Soviet Government, and was the decisive factor in the Labour Party's failure to return to power. Trade relations, however, continued, but these abruptly came to an end when, on Government instructions, the police raided the premises of Arcos Ltd, the trading agency of the Soviet Government in London, in search of a British Government document which, it was alleged, had come improperly into the possession of the agency. The document was not found, but a suspicion that Arcos Ltd was housing spies was said to be supported by the results of the search.

Feeling in Britain during these years was strongly divided. The trade unions and the "left" were in favour of full and good relations with the new socialist State, and this was reflected in the *Daily Herald* and the *Manchester Guardian*. Conservative opinion, although not entirely opposed to trade relations, remained hostile to the Soviet Government.

1928—1939

In the eleven years following the inauguration of the First Five-Year Plan, the Soviet Government, now committed, after a violent internal discussion, to the policy of "socialism in one country," pursued a steady policy of peace and collaboration. The first few years of this period were the years of the world economic crisis, and if the former policy of world revolution had prevailed, a situation in which sixty millions of the world's workers were unemployed might have seemed opportune for trying to implement it. But Trotsky and the other advocates of world revolution had been superseded, denounced, liquidated or forced to fly the country.

The first Five-Year Plan required foreign currency to buy foreign equipment and foreign skill. This meant markets for Russian products that had for the time being to be sold abroad instead of being consumed at home. The Plan also required a period of stability in external relations. The Soviet Government, therefore, embarked on a number of commercial treaties and friendly pacts. It was a propitious time for such activities: the rumblings of the Great War were at last silent and the League of Nations, having accepted Germany as a member, was enjoying its brief hour of prestige. Between 1929 and 1935 Russia concluded pacts of non-aggression with the Baltic States (1932-1933), Finland (1932), France (1932), Poland (1932), Czechoslovakia (1935), Turkey (1929), and Afghanistan (1931). A Pact of Friendship was also agreed upon with Italy in 1933, the year when most of the undertakings were signed. With Germany relations had been exceptionally cordial since 1922 when the two countries, thrown together as discredited parties, had concluded an agreement at Rapallo. This had blossomed into a Treaty of Friendship and Non-Aggression in 1926. During the first Five-Year Plan

trade between the two countries flourished. In fact, a great
deal of equipment essential to the industrialization of the
Soviet Union was provided by Germany.

When the Disarmament Conference opened in Geneva in
1932 the Soviet Union accepted the invitation to attend, and
through her delegate M. Litvinov, then Commissar for Foreign Affairs, advocated at first universal and total disarma-
ament and then a fifty per cent reduction of armaments on
the part of all nations. Two years later, in 1934, the U.S.S.R.
applied for membership of the League of Nations and from
then until 1938 there was no more vigorous advocate of the
policy of collective security than M. Litvinov. The Soviet
Union now stood for an "Anti-Fascist Front."

Since the Soviet championship of League principles has
often been regarded as insincere by critics of Soviet policy, it
is appropriate to point out that collective action by the League
in the 1930's, if it could have been achieved, would have been
in Russia's interest. In 1933 Hitler came to power, having already declared in *Mein Kampf* that the Ukraine provided a
natural *lebensraum* for the German people. His unrestrained
denunciations of Bolshevism, even if intended primarily for
German ears and for propaganda in the western democracies,
were hardly reassuring to the Soviet Government. Japan, in-
vading Manchuria in 1931-1932, brought Japanese troops to
the further side of Russia's frontiers in the Far East. Thus before the Five-Year Plans were completed the Soviet Union
had predatory neighbours on two sides. It seems, therefore,
that the Soviet Union, like other Member States, in support-
ing the League followed a policy which coincided with its
own interests. The mistrust which M. Litvinov failed to
disperse was no doubt derived partly from the old suspicions
and partly from the knowledge that the Soviet press had

hitherto held up the League to scorn and ridicule. One of the difficulties that faces any student of Soviet policy lies in the abruptness with which that policy may be changed to meet a changed situation.

Up to 1935 Russia's policy of collaboration seemed to be achieving some success. In that year the Soviet Pacts of Mutual Assistance with France and with Czechoslovakia were drawn up and were regarded by the countries concerned as a protection against the Nazi menace. In the same year Mr Eden visited Moscow. It was also the year of the Seventh Congress of the Comintern. This was the first meeting since 1928 and its purpose was to lay down a new policy of co-operation with all who stood against fascism. Henceforth Communist parties were not to stand apart but to seek collaboration with other left wing parties and help to form anti-fascist "popular fronts"—a natural corollary to the foreign policy of the Soviet Government.

From 1936, however, Soviet Russia's position weakened. The Anti-Comintern Pact sponsored by Hitler looked more formidable than the alliances linking Russia with the west, especially as Britain had no other bond with Russia than that of fellow member of the League. In the summer of 1936 the Spanish Civil War broke out, and Russia's assistance to the Spanish Government followed the intervention of Italy and Germany on the side of General Franco. This action revived all the old suspicions about world revolution.

Before the Civil War was over Hitler's claim to the Sudeten lands in Czechoslovakia had followed his re-occupation of the Rhineland and annexation of Austria. At Munich the Soviet Union was not invited to send a representative to confer with Mr Chamberlain, M. Daladier and Hitler, although, like France, she had guaranteed to help the Czechs in the event of a German attack. When it is remembered that during the earlier part of 1938 there was a good deal of talk in Germany about an eastward expansion into the Ukraine, it will be seen that Russia's interest lay in withstanding a German thrust to the south-east—that is, through Czechoslovakia.

After Munich it was clear that the Soviet policy of collaboration had been rejected. A *sauve qui peut* situation developed in Europe and the Soviet Union (now embarked on the third Five-Year Plan) was ready in 1939 to try to revive the good relations with Germany which had preceded the Hitler regime. But the first negotiations related entirely to trade. Thus it was hoped to postpone, if not to stop, Hitler's proposed advance into the Ukraine. Before the German Government responded, the German armies invaded Czechoslovakia (March) and thereby disproved Hitler's earlier contention that he only sought to restore Germans to their Fatherland. The British Government, now convinced that Hitler intended to dominate Europe, at once gave a guarantee to Poland and Rumania. It refused as premature the immediate proposal of the Soviet Government for a conference at Bucharest, but a few weeks later began to negotiate with Russia for an Anglo-Soviet Agreement. The Germans were, however, now ready to consider the possibility of a Soviet-German Pact.

From the Soviet point of view a German pact was, for the moment, much more important. It meant buying off the Germans from the Ukraine—at least for the time being; whereas the guarantee which the British had now given to Poland meant that in any case Britain was already pledged to obstruct any German march to Russia through that country.

In August 1939 the Soviet-German Non-Aggression Pact

H

was announced to a startled world. When, a few weeks later, the Germans invaded Poland, the Red Army advanced across the Polish frontier as far as a line which approximated to the old "Curzon Line", but extending further south. The territories thus acquired (and which, for the most part, had been part of the old pre-revolution Russia) were incorporated into the neighbouring Soviet Republics.

The Soviet Government's external policy in the next twelve months showed that they regarded the Pact with Germany as merely a truce. Mutual Assistance Pacts were signed with the Baltic States and certain strategic positions acquired from them. Similar but more susbtantial demands for strategic positions were asked from Finland. These, however, were refused, and the Soviet-Finnish War followed. It was on account of this war that the Soviet Union was expelled from the League of Nations. When the Red Army, after initial setbacks, was victorious, rather more was taken from Finland than had been originally demanded, but the victory was not used to over-rule Finland's independence. In the course of 1940 the Baltic States joined the Soviet Union, under pressure. By these various means the U.S.S.R. prepared her western defences against possible attack. In June 1941 the German invasion took place.

2. DURING THE WAR: A SUMMARY OF EVENTS

The events recorded in this section will fall into their proper perspective with the passage of time. Useful comment can scarcely be made at this stage and in the space available here. Nevertheless, there are three general remarks which should perhaps be made at the outset.

First, Russia has now returned to the councils of Europe as a Great Power. During the twenty years which followed the

Bolshevik Revolution it had become usual not to reckon with her (except as a possible danger), and the extent of her recovery, as well as the solidity of the Soviet regime, was generally under-estimated. The new situation in which the Soviet Union exercises the influence of a leading nation is only new, however, to the present generation; in the nineteenth century Imperial Russia's position as a Great Power was never in dispute. Second, the Soviet Union, largely composed of Slav peoples, shows a special interest in Slav countries, and it seems likely that on the basis of racial kinship she will seek close relations with her Slav neighbours. Third, the Soviet leaders are inflamed by a determination to prevent any further aggression from Germany, or, perhaps, it would be more correct to say, any further fascist aggression. This, in the view of many dispassionate observers, is the predominant motive behind, not only the alliance with the Western Powers, but also the Soviet concern with Eastern and Central Europe.

1941

A few days after the German attack on the Soviet Union, Stalin, in an address to the Soviet Nation, defended the German-Soviet Pact. "By concluding that pact," he said, "we assured to our country peace during eighteen months, as well as an opportunity of getting our forces ready in the event of Germany attacking our country despite the pact."

Mr Churchill had already—within 24 hours of the German invasion—addressed the British people, declaring that, while he did not withdraw his earlier opinions on communism, he recognized Russia as an ally and Britain would fight by her side. The Moscow radio broadcast the speech in Russian, omitting the references to communism. Mr Churchill's declaration was warmly received in Moscow and on July 12 an Agreement for mutual help was signed. A Russian Military Mission arrived in London and a British Military Mission in Moscow. There were also immediate discussions on the supply of war materials from Britain and America.

At the same time the Soviet Government began the process of re-establishing diplomatic relations with all the Allied countries. The first and most important of these was with Poland. On July 30 an Agreement was signed with that country providing for mutual aid in the war against Germany and for the formation of a Polish army in Russia. The army was to be raised from the prisoners and deportees whom the Soviet Government had removed from Poland into the Soviet Union while the previous state of war existed between the two countries. In a Protocol to the Agreement, the Soviet Government granted an amnesty to all Polish citizens detained on Soviet territory.

1942

The first nine months of 1942 were a period of increasing co-operation and goodwill between Soviet Russia and the Allies, to whom the Americans were now formally joined. The war effort in the U.S.S.R. where the Germans had overrun the western territories, was intense, and to the Soviet Trade Union delegates who came to England in January 1943 the British industrial tempo seemed inadequate by comparison. While praising the British people M. Shvernik, the Soviet Trade Union leader, did not scruple to point out that there were unused reserves in this country and that these should be mobilized.

The major event of 1942 in the field of foreign relations was the signing of the Anglo-Soviet Treaty of Alliance in London on May 26. The eight articles embodied agreement on the following matters: (1) every kind of mutual assistance in the war; (2) no negotiations with the existing, or similar, German Government, and no separate peace; (3) a desire to unite with other like-minded States in plans for peace and security after the war; (4) an undertaking to give military help if the enemy should renew the attack on one party after the Armistice; (5) collaboration after the re-establishment of peace for the organization of security and economic prosperity in Europe, taking into account the interests of the United Nations and acting on the principles of no aggrandisement for themselves and no interference in the internal affairs of other States; (6) all possible economic assistance to each other after the war; (7) neither party to take part in any alliance or coalition against the other; (8) the treaty to remain in force for 20 years.

It was categorically stated by Mr Eden and by M. Molotov that the Treaty contained no secret clause. Its signature was the occasion of further discussions on the supply of war material to the Soviet Union, and it was followed by a financial agreement to facilitate these supplies. It also preceded consultations on the combined war strategy. Mr Churchill went to Moscow in August, accompanied by leaders of the fighting services. Mr Harriman and American advisers joined them in consultations with the Russians.

In the autumn of 1942 it became apparent that the Soviet peoples regretted the delay over the opening of the "Second Front" and felt that they were bearing a disproportionate share of the burden of war. Stalin himself, in a letter to a representative of the Associated Press, stated that Allied help to the Soviet Union had little effect in comparison with the aid which the Soviet Union gave to the Allies in drawing upon herself the main enemy forces, and in his review of the war situation on the eve of the anniversary of the revolution, he attributed the German successes in South-West Russia to the fact that no second European front existed to draw off some of the enemy's strength. Similar statements were made on later occasions and were reflected in the press up to the time of the Moscow Conference (October 1943).

1943

The year 1943 brought a deterioration and finally a breach of relations between the Soviet Union and Poland—this will be dealt with in the consecutive account of Soviet-Polish differences which is given later. The same year also saw three events which improved the relations between the U.S.S.R. and her two chief Allies. The first of these was the abolition of the Comintern in May. This was first accomplished by a resolution of the Executive Committee in which the national sections of the International were declared free from the rules and the decisions of the Congresses which had hitherto bound them. The formal dissolution occurred on June 10 after messages of agreement had been received from the thirty-one constituent sections. On May 30 M. Stalin stated that the dissolution exposed the Hitlerite lie that Russia intended to intervene and Bolshevize the nations.

The other two events were the Moscow and Tehran Conferences. The Moscow Conference opened on October 19 and was attended by the foreign secretaries of Russia, the U.S.A. and Great Britain, with M. Molotov presiding. The chiefs-of-staff of the three countries were also present. The Conference issued four Declarations: (1) binding the signatories to mutual consultation until some machinery for general security was set up; (2) undertaking to restore free institutions to Italy as soon as the Commander-in-Chief in

Italy deemed that this could be done; (3) stating the annexation of Austria by Hitler in 1938 to be null and void and undertaking to restore that country's independence; (4) announcing that at the time of the armistice Germans responsible for atrocities would be sent to the countries concerned for punishment.

The Tehran Conference was held from November 28 until December 1 and was attended by M. Stalin, Mr Roosevelt, Mr Churchill, and their respective Service Chiefs. Its purpose may be deduced from the following extract from the joint declaration: "We have concerted our plans for the destruction of the German forces . . . We fully recognize the supreme responsibility resting on us and all United Nations to make a peace which will command the goodwill of the overwhelming masses of the people of the world and banish the scourge of war for many generations."

After the Conference had concluded, an important article in *Izvestia* explained that the pronouncement on Austria did not mean that Russia envisaged Austria as part of a Danubian Confederation. On the contrary, Russia remained opposed to any grouping of Central and Eastern European States.

The Tehran Conference followed a conference in Cairo between Mr Roosevelt, Generalissimo Chiang Kai-Shek and Mr Churchill. The Soviet Government was unable to join in Allied consultation with the Chinese leader since Russia was not at war with Japan. The Neutrality Agreement with Japan, signed in April 1941, still held good, although there had been moments of tension between the countries.

1944

During 1944 there were various developments, most of them arising out of the military successes of Russia and her

Allies. In the early spring there were negotiations for an armistice with Finland. The Soviet terms required the internment of German forces on Finnish territory and the re-establishment of the 1940 Treaty (which had concluded the earlier Russo-Finnish War). The questions of reparations, the demobilization of the Finnish Army and the Petsamo area were to be left for subsequent negotiations. After some delay the Finnish Government announced that they found technical difficulties and a threat to Finnish independence in the way of acceptance of these terms and refused them. There had been virtually no criticism of the terms in the British or American press. Finland finally came out of the war in September, when an Armistice was concluded between the Finnish Government on the one hand and the Soviet and British Governments on the other. The terms were very similar to those originally proposed.

In September, Rumania asked for an armistice. The peace terms included a recognition by Rumania of the incorporation of Bessarabia and Bukhovina into the U.S.S.R. With Bulgaria the Soviet Union had not hitherto been at war although that country had served the enemy's cause by permitting the Germans to use Bulgarian ports and Bulgarian territory for operations against the Soviet Union. In April, however, the Soviet Government called upon the Bulgarian Government to refuse further German support. An exchange of Notes between the two countries followed and since Bulgaria took no action the Soviet Union finally declared a state of war (September 5). This, however, only lasted a few days, as on September 9 the Bulgarian Government asked for an armistice.

A strong line, although sometimes restricted to official pronouncements, was taken towards certain other Governments.

In February an Agreement on the lines of the Czechoslovak-Soviet Treaty, offered by the Yugoslav Government, was refused by the Soviet Union on the grounds that the situation in Yugoslavia was too unsettled. (In the spring of 1942 the Yugoslav Government had refused an agreement proposed by Moscow.) In October the Soviet Government demanded oil concessions in Iran. When the Iran Government refused to discuss the matter until the war was over the Soviet Vice-Commissar of Foreign Affairs, who had arrived in Tehran, warned the Iran Government that it was steering a course which would make for bad relations between the two countries and in the resulting crisis a new Iranian Government was formed. At the end of the European War the matter still awaited settlement. Throughout 1944 the Soviet press attacked the neutral countries, particularly Spain, declaring that they were helping the enemy under the mask of neutrality. In November the Soviet Government refused an overture from Switzerland for the re-establishment of diplomatic relations. The reason given was the "hostile and pro-fascist policy" pursued against the Soviet Union.

The Soviet attitude towards the Badoglio Government which was functioning in Italy during the early months of 1944 seemed somewhat in contrast to all this. The Soviet Union established direct relations with this Government by sending an accredited representative at the beginning of April. About the same time an article in *Izvestia* contradicted any notion that this unilateral action should be interpreted as Soviet approval of the provisional Italian Government, and implied that Britain and America were not only responsible for the character of that government, but also that they had acted without consultation with the Soviet Union.

During 1944 the first steps were taken towards building

a future structure of peace and international collaboration. At the I.L.O. conference in Philadelphia the Soviet Union was not represented, although it was the earnest desire of the Conference that she should send a delegation. At Dumbarton Oaks (September-October) she was naturally one of the four signatory Powers who sponsored the "tentative proposals" for a new World Organization. It was known that the Soviet Government was strongly in favour of vesting the authority of the new Security Organization in the Great Powers, and that it stood for what came to be known as the "veto". According to the Soviet newspaper, *The War and the Working Class*, the Russians held that the responsibility for a durable peace rested on those countries whose armies might bring about victory. In general the line taken by the Soviet Union in this connection showed a not unnatural anxiety lest Russia should again be in an isolated position.

At the Civil Aviation meeting in Chicago, which was held shortly after the Conference at Dumbarton Oaks, the Soviet Union, although expected to participate, was absent, refusing to sit down at the conference table with Switzerland, Spain and Portugal on the grounds that these Governments had been hostile towards her for many years.

The year concluded with a Treaty of Alliance and Mutual Assistance between the U.S.S.R. and the French Republic, following on the recognition of the French Provisional Government.

One other event of the year must be mentioned in this chapter, although already referred to in a previous chapter. This was the change in the constitution which gave the individual Republics of the U.S.S.R. separate Commissariats for Defence and Foreign Affairs. This change gave emphasis to the independent status of the constituent Republics, always insisted on by the Soviet Government, and paved the way for a request made at the Yalta Conference, in February 1945, that two of the republics, Ukraine and White Russia, should have separate membership in the proposed new World Organization.

This request became public as the San Francisco Conference met and it was acceded to by a large majority of the delegates.

POLAND

Since the Soviet Union's relations with Poland gave rise to a basic disagreement between the U.S.S.R. and her two major allies during the last two years of the European War, the issues must be briefly recapitulated.

The opening month of 1943 saw a deterioration in Soviet-Polish relations. The Poles had complained that the Russians had been unco-operative in the process of releasing Polish prisoners and internees; the Russians had complained that the Polish army, which was to have been formed in Russia to fight on the Russian front, had been removed to Iran. Both sides objected to unfriendly articles in the national press of the other country. But the fundamental issue for the moment was the question of the frontier. In February the Polish Government in London stated that they only recognized the pre-1939 frontier (as established by the Treaty of Riga in 1921). To this the Soviet News Agency replied, accusing the Poles of failing to recognize the rights of the Ukrainians and White Russians. Both sides invoked the Atlantic Charter. Continuing the controversy, the Polish Government declared that until the Pact with Germany in 1939 the Russians had never questioned the Treaty of Riga and that this Russo-German Pact was cancelled by the Polish-Soviet

Agreement of July 30, 1941. The plebiscite which had been ordered by the Soviet occupation authorities in Eastern Poland in 1939 was, according to the Polish view, contrary to international law, and its results (the acceptance of Soviet citizenship by the people of Eastern Poland) were therefore invalid.

In April these recriminations reached fever pitch as the result of a German announcement that 8,000 bodies of Polish officers had been found buried near Smolensk. The Germans declared that the officers had been murdered by the Russians. The Polish Government appeared to accept the German statement and pointed out that 8,300 officers who had been imprisoned in Eastern Poland under the Soviet occupation had been missing since 1940. It announced that it would ask the Red Cross to investigate. An immediate reply on the Moscow radio declared this to be a "frame-up", and asked how the bodies and their accompanying documents could have been preserved. In the Soviet view the Germans had murdered the Polish officers and the Russians charged the Polish Government with conniving with the Germans. They declared that similar campaigns had been launched in Polish and German newspapers, and that the purpose of the Polish Government was to bring pressure on the Soviet Government to yield their western territories. The Soviet Government would not agree to a Red Cross investigation on territory held by the Germans. Finally, the Soviet Government severed relations with Poland.

In a personal letter to the British press on May 5, M. Stalin stated that his Government wished to see a strong independent Poland after the war, and that he desired that relations between Russia and Poland should be based on solid good-neighbourliness and mutual respect—or, if the Poles wished, on an alliance of mutual assistance against Germany.

Meanwhile, a Union of Polish Patriots came to the fore in the Soviet Union. It was opposed to the Polish Government on various grounds, including the Government's decision to remove the Polish army to Iran. The Union's policy was one of full support for the Soviet Government, and by an arrangement with the Soviet authorities it formed a Polish division to fight with the Red Army.

The re-entry of the Red Army into Eastern Poland at the beginning of 1944 brought about a sharp interchange of notes between the Soviet and Polish Governments. Now that the disputed territories were in the process of being liberated by Soviet forces, the question of the frontier naturally became acute. The Polish Government in London claimed sovereignty over Eastern Poland, but the Soviet Government remained adamant in insisting that the matter had been properly settled on a racial basis by the plebiscite of 1939. The desire for a strong and independent Poland, bound by friendship to Russia, was repeated by Moscow, and it was suggested that Poland might join the Treaty which had just been concluded with Czechoslovakia, binding that country and the Soviet Union to mutual assistance in the war and collaboration in the peace. It was also said that Poland must be reborn, not by the seizure of lands in the east, but by the restoration of territory taken from her by the Germans, but belonging to her from time immemorial (that is, Pomerania, Silesia, and East Prussia).

Shortly afterwards the Union of Polish Patriots in Russia announced that a National Council had been democratically elected in liberated Poland. From this assembly a Committee of National Liberation was subsequently formed—commonly known at the time as the Lublin Committee. The National

Council declared this Committee to be the sole source of authority in Poland and denounced the Polish Government in London as illegal, because based on the "Fascist Constitution of 1935."

In July, when M. Mikolajczik was on his way to discuss matters in Moscow, it was announced that the Soviet Government and the Lublin Committee had made an agreement about the relationship between the Soviet High Command and the Polish administration. This event prevented M. Mikolajczik, on arrival in Moscow, from entering upon any serious negotiations, as he felt obliged to return to consult his colleagues in London. The situation was critical because of the military situation in Warsaw. There, the people of the city, acting under the orders of General Bor (the commander-in-chief recognized by the London Poles) had risen to attack the occupying German Army. The Soviet forces were fast closing in, and the Warsaw Poles had been spurred on to action not only by their Underground Movement (under the control of the Polish Government in London) but also by the appeals of the Union of Polish Patriots broadcast from radio stations in the Soviet Union. However, according to an article in *Pravda* on August 19 the Soviet Government had not wished for an uprising of the people and considered it doomed to failure, since the resistance movement was relatively ill-armed and German strength heavily concentrated. It did, in fact, fail, although to relieve the shortage of food and arms British, American and Polish aircraft (without Soviet co-operation) flew in to drop supplies. Discussion in October between Mr Churchill, Mr Eden, M. Stalin and representatives of both the Polish Government in London and the Lublin Committee, failed to find a solution. M. Mikolajczik resigned the premiership, and in the beginning of 1945 the Soviet Government, by unilateral action, recognized the Lublin Committee as the Provisional Government of Poland.

Poland was one of the main topics of discussion at the Yalta Conference in February 1945. According to the Declaration issued by Mr Churchill, Mr Roosevelt and Marshal Stalin, a new situation had been created as the result of the complete liberation of the country by the Red Army. The existing Provisional Government in Poland was to be broadened by the inclusion of democratic leaders from both inside and outside the country, and the enlarged Government was to be called the Polish Provisional Government of National Unity. To bring about this reorganization the Soviet Foreign Minister (M. Molotov) and the British and American Ambassadors in Moscow would form a Commission to consult with Polish leaders.

Later, however, it appeared that the Soviet Government interpreted this decision to mean that the existing Provisional Government in Poland was to be the nucleus of the new government with a few additions, whereas the British and American authorities envisaged a more complete reorganization. The whole situation remained obscure up to the time of the meeting of the San Francisco Conference.[1] A few days before the Conference met the Soviet Government announced that it had concluded a Treaty of Friendship, Mutual Assistance and Post-war Co-operation with the Provisional Go-

---

[1] On June 16, 1945, M. Mikolajczik, former head of the Polish Government in London and a member of the Peasant Party, and M. Stanczyk, member of the Socialist Party, arrived in Moscow, where a delegation from the Polish Provisional Government in Warsaw had also arrived. After negotiations lasting just under a fortnight, the formation of a new Polish Government of National Unity was announced, with M. Osubka-Morawski as Prime Minister, M. Mikolajczik as Vice-Premier and Minister of Agriculture and M. Stanczyk as Minister of Labour and Social Welfare. This new Polish Government was recognized early in July by Great Britain and the United States.

vernment. The Soviet Union also asked that the Provisional Government should be represented at the San Francisco Conference. Britain and the United States did not agree and the proposal, when put to the Conference by M. Molotov, was not carried.

1945

In the spring of 1945 the Soviet Government concluded a Treaty of Friendship with Yugoslavia. It also denounced the Neutrality Pact with Japan which had been made in April 1941. M. Molotov pointed out that in the changed situation, in which Japan was aiding Germany and making war against the allies of the Soviet Union, the Pact had lost its meaning.

The chief event of this spring, however, was the meeting of the United Nations Conference at San Francisco, to which reference has already been made. Although the Soviet Government had previously appointed the Soviet Ambassador in Washington as its representative, at the urgent request of the new American President, Mr Truman, it agreed to send M. Molotov. The Soviet Union thus participated in the Conference with the full authority of a sponsoring Power.